Connect, Communicate, and Profit

Build Successful Business Relationships Online

by D'vorah Lansky

*"The most important thing in any relationship is not
what you get, but what you give."*

Eleanor Roosevelt

August 2010

ISBN 978-0-9651975-1-9

Published by:
Desktop Wings Inc.
700 East Walnut Street
Perkasie, PA 18944
215-453-9312

Dedication

To my mom who was my best friend and biggest cheerleader. I miss you Mom, thanks for reminding me to "smell the roses".

To my Grandma Rose who taught us to set our goals high and go for our dreams.

To my darling son Ranan: your love for literature has always been an inspiration. Thank you for spurring me on. Now it's time for you to live your dream my son; spread your wings and fly.

This book is for you!

Testimonials

"Let me make this simple. If you want to build a huge network of people who think about you, care about you, trust you and most importantly, refer you...but you only have a few minutes a day to do it, then you need to buy this book **today** and devour it. What more can I say?"

David Frey, CEO, Marketing Best Practices, www.MarketingBestPractices.com

"If you want to profit from your people skills, D'vorah gives you a step-by-step roadmap to reach your goals through the power of relationships. Highly recommended!"

Noah St. John, Ph.D., No. 1 Bestselling author of *The Secret Code of Success,* www.SecretCodeBook.com

"From A-Z—articles to videos and everything in between—this book delivers on the tips and techniques with specific how-tos, clear instructions, and ideas for effectively communicating your messages authentically using relationship marketing. Packed with useful and valuable content, this is a definitive resource that you will refer to over and over again."

Felicia J. Slattery, M.A., M.Ad.Ed., Author of *Cash in on Communication,* www.CommunicationTransformation.com

"D'vorah teaches the how to of 'connecting' and the how to of 'profiting from your connections' with passion, clarity and simplicity. Whatever your industry, whatever your walk of life, this book will prove to be a powerful tool for your success. Buy it now and profit from your investment."

Rick Angel, Esq., Legal Advisor, Commercial Real Estate Transactions, Lecturer, and Author, www.RickAngel.com

"Relationship building has always been critical in any business, but today it's even more important because of the way we now communicate with one another. Text messages, social media, and email have digitized much of our social interaction, often leaving it cold, empty, and scattered. However, this book provides a wonderful roadmap for combining the speed of today's communication with the effective relationship building methods of yesterday. This is a great book for any business owner looking to generate more sales, referrals, and connections in a given marketplace."

Stu McLaren, Co-Founder, WishList Products, www.WishListMember.com

"The next best thing to hiring D'vorah Lansky as your relationship marketing wizard is to read her book and apply her expertise to your business. Be prepared for explosive growth!"

Marge and Bruce Brown, Co-owners, Quantum Results Coaching, www.QuantumResultsCoaching.com

"*Connect, Communicate, and Profit* is a comprehensive book that walks you through a step-by-step, proven process to build successful business relationships online. D'vorah is a master, and I have personally benefitted from her vast knowledge and expertise."

Marge Piccini, Founder and CEO of MVP & Company and co-author of *Incredible Business,* www.MargePiccini.com

"D'vorah is indeed a 'wizard' when it comes to relationship marketing. In this book she shares with you the magic formula that has helped her to build a successful business by nurturing relationships."

Reno Lovison, Author of *Turn Your Business Card Into Business,* www.BusinessCardToBusiness.com

"D'vorah Lansky really is the 'wizard' of relationship marketing! Her practical guidance in this book gives you more than a few strategies to apply to your own business; it gives you a whole new perspective on marketing. People are inundated with advertisements (traditional marketing) all day long. This book tells you how to make your business different enough (for you) to stand out and become the top go-to person for your product or business. And who couldn't use customers that bring higher profits?"

Kristen J. Eckstein, Imagine! Studios, LLC, The Ultimate Book Coach, www.UltimateBookCoach.com

"D'vorah Lansky's book is a must read if you have any interest in taking your business online. She shares fifteen years of learning in a concise and easy way to use. It's so practical and provides action steps and resources all the way through to the end. Keep it on your computer desk and you'll be referring to it again and again for its great ideas!"

Drew and Vicky Riggio, LaunchPad Coaching, LLC, www.LaunchPadCoaching.com

"The content provides a valuable survey of Internet marketing methods, offering a wealth of information and recommended resources. The material is very practical so you can start using it right away. The depth of content also offers plenty of room to grow, so that you continue to benefit from it as you evolve your skills."

Joan Pagano, Author of *Strength Training for Women*, www.JoanPaganoFitness.com

"I find D'vorah's content and teaching style so simple and "absorbable." As a psychotherapist and an intuitive life coach, I tend to be extraordinarily right brained. I needed the lessons to build upon each other, which D'vorah's content easily does. She is optimistic, full of belief in your skills, and the unique gift of each person. This shows in her writing style and also her personal contact. It doesn't get much better than this!"

Sharon Massoth, LCSW, CPC,
Intuitive View Coaching,
www.SharonMassoth.com

"I found D'vorah's programs extremely useful in helping me bring my businesses to the next level. The tremendous amount of information she provides on the use of Web sites, blogs, and social networking, as well as her proposals for the use of audio/video presentations as both educational and passive income-producing vehicles, are relevant, timely, and cutting edge for today's businesses. There is substantial and significant content to her programs and most certainly countless valuable ideas for businesses of all kinds. I have followed through on many of her ideas and plan to go forward with even more, as I have seen growth in my businesses since those implementations."

Dory Dzinski, LPC, NCC, Nationally Certified Licensed Professional Counselor, www.DoryDzinski.com

"This is a powerful book! I learned important Internet marketing strategies that were simple and free! D'vorah is an inspired teacher who delivers high content and high quality information. I highly recommend this book for solopreneurs who need to transition away from the 'old school' marketing techniques."

Cheryl Jones-Reardon, MA, The Mindful Path, www.TheMindfulPath.com

Foreword

If you wear the marketing hat in your company, then reading this book and taking action on what's inside could make the difference between thriving and merely surviving in the years ahead.

As you may have noticed, we are currently in the middle of a significant paradigm shift in the way customers and businesses interact.

Hang on to the old ways, and watch the inevitable decline of your business. Embrace the new methods of relationship marketing online, and position yourself for higher revenues and levels of profitability.

Never before have small business owners like you and I enjoyed such a level playing field when it comes to attracting customers. Equipped with the strategies contained in this book, you can essentially eliminate the need for costly advertising methods that not only break the bank, but are becoming increasingly ineffective.

This is not a temporary, reversible trend. If you look closely you can easily see the writing on the wall.

- In 2010, Pepsi shocked the advertising universe by **not** advertising in the Super Bowl **for the first time in 23 years**. Instead, they're using online relationship building strategies to build greater loyalty and increase market share.

- The top 10 websites in the English speaking world are Google, Facebook, YouTube, Yahoo, Windows Live, Wikipedia, Blogger, MSN, Twitter, and WordPress (according to Alexa). All are based solely on the exchange of information in a customer-centered environment. In fact, **half of these** (Facebook, YouTube, Blogger, Twitter, and WordPress) **are completely based on information generated by users like you and me – for free!**
- A survey by the Nielsen Company in April 2009 asked more than 25,000 people from over 50 countries which forms of advertising they trust most. The categories that were scored as *"completely trust"* or *"somewhat trust"* may surprise you:
  o **Recommendations from people known: 90%**
  o **Consumer opinions posted online: 70%**
  o Brand (company-owned) websites: 70%
  o TV advertising: 62%
  o Newspaper advertising: 61%
  o Search engine results ads: 41%
  (Source: Nielsen.com)

So if consumer-driven research and word of mouth marketing are driving the information economy, how can the busy entrepreneur stand out in a noisy marketplace?

By becoming the obvious solution to the specific problems that customers face.

And that happens fastest through the consistent and strategic use of relationship marketing.

Like others, I'm sure you've heard about social media, personal branding, blogging, etc. But putting all the pieces together remains a struggle for so many. Why is it so difficult?

For one thing, many who attempt to master their own marketing while trying to run their business at the same time often suffer from "shiny object syndrome." Hopping from one magic bullet to the next, most fail to realize any real gains from this type of marketing because they lack these three important things:

- patience and persistence to finish what they start,
- clear steps to implement the different tactics,
- and a comprehensive integration of the essential elements of online marketing.

Connect, Communicate, and Profit gives you the last two of these components, as well as the confidence to supply your own patience and persistence.

Inside the following chapters, you'll find the same proven action steps successful professionals and entrepreneurs are using while their behind-the-times competitors hang on to obsolete and expensive forms of marketing.

More importantly, D'vorah makes it easy for you to implement these strategies.

Forget the arduous process of trial and error that your competition is relying on to figure it all out. D'vorah has done all the research for you, and provides you with the prioritized steps and cost-effective resources right here in this book.

Enjoy the journey!

Bob Jenkins, Author of *Take Action, Revise Later,* www.BobTheTeacher.com

P.S. Let me know how you're putting D'vorah's strategies into action with a post to me (@BobTheTeacher) on Twitter!

Table of Contents

Introduction

In today's busy world, where things move quickly and technology is king, it is essential to have a vibrant and interactive online presence. There are a variety of ways you can acquire the information and skill set to accomplish this. In *Connect, Communicate, and Profit* you will be presented with a comprehensive overview and related action steps to help you master key areas of Internet marketing.

This book is designed for small business professionals and entrepreneurs who want to market online or know that they need to be marketing online but aren't sure where to begin.

Ask yourself, do you want to:

- Get exposure for your business and your Web site?
- Learn the basics of social networking and understand how it can have a positive impact on your business?
- Develop and enhance your online presence and marketing campaigns?

If you answered "yes" to any of these questions, then this book is for you! After reading each chapter you will better understand the basics of Internet marketing and how to develop offline and online marketing techniques for the entrepreneur who wants to flourish in today's Internet-driven business environment.

In *Connect, Communicate, and Profit,* you will be presented with the strategies and techniques needed to get you up to speed on the basics of Internet marketing and how to create a bridge between your online and offline networking and business-building practices.

It has been said that more of our message is conveyed via body language and vocal intonation than via the actual words that we use. In addition to in-person networking, there are many ways that you can share your voice intonation and presence with your online community. This can be primarily accomplished through audio and video technology. We will go into great detail about both of these areas in this book.

Connect, Communicate, and Profit presents several powerful and effective relationship marketing strategies. We will discuss branding strategies, time management, blogging, social networking, in-person networking, greeting card marketing, developing a following and sharing your message via teleseminars, monetizing your expertise, and video marketing.

Whether you have a brick and mortar business or an online business, there are certain basic principles of relationship marketing that, when applied, will serve to help you grow your network, build awareness of your brand, and position yourself as an expert in your field.

Relationship marketing is focusing on building relationships with your prospects, clients, and your network with the intention of strengthening connections and "selling" **yourself,** not your products or services. Through relationship marketing you are presenting your authentic self and focusing on what you can do to be of help or service to others.

By developing a multi-pronged approach to networking that includes an integrated online and offline networking strategy, you will put yourself in front of more people and build relationships, alliances, and joint venture partnerships.

While this book will primarily focus on building business relationships online, we will be discussing key factors and tips for in-person networking as well. Nothing replaces the effectiveness and impact created with in-person networking. Networking online is not meant to replace this traditional approach, but rather to enhance it. There is nothing like face-to-face interaction.

Why I Wrote This Book

When people find out about my professional experience and vast knowledge of Internet marketing, the most common comment I get is "We need to get together so you can teach me everything you know." For a while I would meet with people one-on-one, and then I realized that there is a great thirst for knowledge for Internet marketing and that I had an important message to deliver. Thus I developed a course called "Internet Marketing on a Shoestring." By offering a course, I realized that I would be able to share this information with a wider audience and thus help them gain a working knowledge of Internet marketing. Writing a book is another way for me to share this important information with even more people.

Connect, Communicate, and Profit is the result of more than fifteen years' experience in marketing online, along with an in-depth study of Internet marketing and in-person networking through my involvement with various Chambers of Commerce as well as BNI (Business Network International) groups. Over the past fifteen years I have spent thousands of hours learning and applying the techniques that I present in this book. I realize that the average business professional does not have this kind of time to devote to learning online marketing strategies, but I am a person who loves to learn new things and wants to help others by sharing my knowledge so they can benefit from the information.

I love showing people how to connect online and build a deeper relationship with others in their local community so that when they see each other at local events, they will have a stronger bond and connection. This book is the result of that passion.

I know what it's like to invest hundreds of hours into learning specific aspects of Internet marketing and I realize that while most people don't have this kind of time to invest, they know that they need this information. In *Connect, Communicate, and Profit*, I will give you an overview of key Internet marketing strategies. I make it easy to understand each step, and follow with suggested action steps for each strategy. I designed these action steps to help you get up to speed on the foundation of these strategies. By reading and applying the information in this book and applying the suggested action steps, you will be able to develop a comprehensive online and offline relationship marketing strategy for your business.

What is Relationship Marketing?

If you were to Google the term "relationship marketing," you would find a wide range of definitions. The same would hold true if you were to take a cross section of people who are actively involved in relationship marketing and ask them what they do. You would hear a slightly different definition from each of them, because even though the concept has been around for centuries, relationship marketing is a new and budding field in today's business environment. The bottom line is that relationship marketing is about marketing second and building relationships first. People want to do business with people they know, like, and trust.

I was reminded of this recently when I was walking through a bookstore and overheard a conversation. Someone said, "I don't care how professional he is. If I don't like the guy, I'm not going to do business with him." That is the essence of relationship marketing.

Relationship marketing produces raving fans who refer you to other people without your even asking. It's about building a strong community of people, who come to see you as a go-to person because they know that you care about them and they know that you're knowledgeable. The reason you want to know about relationship marketing is because it's the key to growing your business. By building relationships with people, they're going to want to know you, they're going to want to refer you, and they're going to want to do business with you.

While it seems like common sense that this is how business should be done, this is not the norm. While "info-mercial" sales tactics may seem to work, you'll sell more products and services and increase your repeat customers and referrals by connecting with your market. People want to buy from people, not from a faceless corporation.

In order for people to get to know, like, and trust you, you need to find effective ways to connect with them and bring value to them, and thus begin to build a relationship with them. There are a variety of ways that you can build relationships, trust and credibility with your audience. First and foremost, become known as a "giver" and someone who cares about others.

The Oldest Form of Marketing on the Planet

To put relationship marketing in perspective with your own life, think back to when you have needed the services of a plumber or painter. Did you flip through the phone book and make a random phone call, or did you call someone you knew and ask for a referral to someone that person could highly recommend, someone they had a relationship with?

Doing business with people with whom we've built a relationship or with people who come highly recommended by people we have a relationship with is a big piece of relationship marketing.

There are many reasons to practice relationship marketing:

- Relationship marketing is more enjoyable than traditional marketing. By building relationships, you are building friendships and building your network.
- By helping people in your network, by referring them to others, and, when

appropriate, being available to brainstorm ideas with them, you will ensure that they're going to want to know you and potentially want to do business with you.

- Relationship marketing is the type of marketing that will not only bring more value to your business but will bring a sense of purpose to what you do.

Giving To Give

BNI, the world's largest referral organization, has a motto: "Givers Gain". Relationship marketing falls into this category. By giving to give, not giving to get or with thought of what you will gain, you become a valuable ally. Have you ever met people that you've come to admire and trust and, truth be told, it didn't matter what they were selling, you wanted to do business with them?

Relationship marketing is about reaching out and touching your potential client. As a small business owner or entrepreneur, you truly are the heart of your business. When potential clients come to know you on a personal level, they will consider you an ally and want to buy from you. To truly leverage relationship marketing to its full extent, you want to network in person as well as online and find a way to make a connection between the two. In the chapter on social networking and in-person networking, you will find several examples of how you can make this work.

Building Relationships with Greeting Card Marketing

People do not want to be sold, but they do want to buy. So why should they buy from you? People want to buy from people they like. You might buy a car one time from a person, but if that person doesn't keep in touch with you and let you know that they appreciate you, what's the likelihood of you buying another car from them?

On the other hand, what if that person sent you a card with a picture of you in front of your new car saying, "I hope you are enjoying your new car"? Or "Be sure to stop by for a free car wash when you are in the neighborhood"? What if they went on to keep in touch with you through the years and sent you a card on the anniversary of the date you purchased your car? This is relationship marketing. It's appreciating others, letting them know you care and making sure you come to mind when they have the need for your product or service.

Traditional marketing consists of newspaper ads, Yellow Page ads, even Internet ads or Google ads, but they don't have that personal touch. There are a lot of ways you can touch people. Sending a greeting card is just one of them, but it sets you apart in that people have something from you that is not trying to sell them something, but rather is an expression of your appreciation. By appreciating others you're going to grow your business.

When I moved to my new town in 2005, my back became sore from all the lifting and moving of boxes. I decided to treat myself to a massage. The first step I took was to reach for the Yellow Pages, since I was new in town and didn't have local friends to ask for a referral. I selected a local massage therapist and went to her for a massage. A few days later I received a beautiful card with lilacs on it. I opened it up and it said, "Thanks for coming by. Be sure to tell your friends and family where I am because I'll be happy to take care of them, too." That's what I remember from the card. I thought to myself, "What a wasted opportunity" and threw the card into the trash. I didn't care how pretty the cover was, since it seemed to be all about her wanting to grow her business with no apparent interest in or appreciation for me or my patronage.

What if, instead, that person had said something like this: "Thank you so much for taking the time to come and pamper yourself. It was a joy to meet you. The next time you would like some nurturing I would love to be able to offer you a massage. In fact, here's a coupon that you can enjoy on your next visit. I know you're new to town. If you have any questions or need any recommendations, give me a call. I'm happy to help."

A message like that would have demonstrated that she cared about me and appreciated my business. Instead her card gave the impression that she cared more about future sales than in developing relationships with her clients. Thus, I decided to find another massage therapist. I think a lot of business is lost because people don't let their clients know that they truly care about them.

I'm the type of person who will go out of her way to connect with people, to help introduce them to others and bring them to events. When you build a relationship you're not just building a friendship, you're building trust. Once trust is built with someone, you can confidently refer business his or her way. You've built a relationship with someone you know will take good care of your friend or your family member. Thus, it becomes easy to refer them.

Traditional Direct Mail versus Heartfelt Appreciation

Let's talk about two different types of mailings that business people send out and you decide which type would be most effective. Ask yourself, are you sending give-to-give or give-to-get types of mailings to your clients? A give-to-get mailing is something that many professionals send out, thinking that they are touching their clients in a positive way. Here's an example: "Hi. I'm your local salesperson. Here is a recipe card for you to enjoy. I'm never too busy to take care of your referrals." Why would I want to send them referrals or want to do business with them? This type of card is not a card of appreciation that encourages relationship building. It is a give-to-get type of card. They gave me a recipe card, but they want to get my referrals. They haven't built credibility or trust. Why should I give them my referrals?

A give-to-give card could be from someone you met at a Chamber of Commerce event saying something like, "It was nice meeting you at the Chamber of Commerce networking event. I enjoyed our conversation and look forward to seeing you again soon." That's a give-to-give card. That type of heartfelt card would certainly get my attention. The sender is a person that I'd want to get to know better and who knows where that could lead. This could end up turning into business, a friendship, an introduction, or a warm entry the next time I go to an event.

So there's a big difference between give-to-give and give-to-get. Before you send out an email or a card, stop and read it as if the message were addressed to you and pay attention to how it makes you feel.

I can't stress enough how much effective marketing depends on relationships. Businesses that grow the quickest truly understand this concept. They focus on building the relationship and not on the sales or profits. So the bottom line is if you focus on relationships first, your business is going to grow so much faster than if you are only interested in making that sale.

The Essentials of Relationship Marketing Online

In today's business environment you really need to be able to effectively combine online and offline marketing. Even if you are really good at one or the other, you need the combination of both.

The business professional who has a vibrant brick and mortar business but does not have a Web presence is creating a handicap for that business. The day of relying on the Yellow Pages and newspaper ads as the most effective way to bring in new clients is long gone. Your clients are likely turning to the Internet to do their initial research. If your business does not show up in their Google search, you are missing out on a lot of potential business.

At the same time, if you have an Internet-based business and you are not networking in person or doing anything to reach out through direct mail to thank and appreciate your clients, you are leaving a lot of money and potential repeat business on the table.

Even the savviest Internet marketers who have live events and online courses would benefit from keeping in touch with people through direct mail. In this way they will have the opportunity to stay at top of mind and get something in the hands of their prospects, clients, and networking contacts to let them know they care.

I remember the first time that I received something from an Internet marketer. I had purchased an online downloadable product and the person I purchased from sent me a DVD and a card in the mail. It caused me to sit up and take notice of this teacher and I wanted to know more about who he was and what other courses he might teach. This thought came into being because of how this teacher reached out to let me know that he cared and that connecting with students and clients was important to him. I was so impressed that I started to visit his blog and keep up with him on the social networks.

Food for Thought

Just like in-person networking, building relationships with people online is not about trying to sell them "stuff." Instead, sell them on "you" and create raving fans.

- As an example, think about the emails you get and the messages you get on the social networks. Which are the ones you read and which are the ones that you delete?
- How do you feel about the person whose list you signed up on, with the expectation of receiving informative content, along with product recommendations, and you discover that just about every email coming from that person is about them trying to sell you something?
- One of the best ways to become known, liked, and trusted is to become an authority in your field and find ways to share your knowledge and expertise with others.

As you apply these principles of relationship marketing and incorporate them into your online networking and business building strategies, you will be broadening the foundation of your business. In the following chapters I will present you with powerful online and offline relationship marketing techniques and strategies for growing your business.

At the end of each chapter you will find Action Steps that will allow you to apply the strategies discussed along with a list of resources mentioned in that chapter. In addition, at the end of this book you will find details about a free companion course that you'll receive as a thank-you gift for purchasing this book. In that course, I will show you how to connect, communicate, and profit by developing your online platform.

Take things one step at a time and you will be effectively marketing online in record time.

Here's to your success!

Dvorah Lansky

Getting Organized and Developing an Online Branding Strategy

An essential part of online marketing is building your brand and creating a branded image. By developing your branded image and name brand recognition, you give people the chance to get to know you, and in time they will learn to trust you and look forward to hearing from you. As you brand yourself on the Internet, keep this fact in mind and you will benefit greatly.

Another essential ingredient for successful online marketing is effective time management. By being careful with your time and employing a few powerful techniques, you will be able to accomplish a great deal. I'll address time management first, as all other tasks really flow from effective use of time.

Time Management

If you manage your time properly you are going to have more energy and you are going to get more done. You're also going to be able to give more because you're not going to be stressed over a project that you have due. Manage your time more efficiently and you will be more focused. For example, when you are working on setting up your Web site or interacting on the social networks or you are at an in-person networking event, you won't become distracted thinking of all the things that you should be doing; instead, you'll be able to focus on being present where you are.

A big part of time management is delegation. Delegation will not only free up more of your time to be more productive, but it will also use someone else's expertise in a particular area that you may not be proficient in. Typically when you prioritize people over paper, you will be focusing on income-producing activities and projects that are the best use of your time. For example, you might be really good at entering data, filing papers, cleaning your home or office, packaging products, or filling orders, but those tasks can easily be delegated to someone else so that you can focus on things like delivering a teleseminar, writing an article, or coaching your clients.

Perhaps you feel guilty about delegating tasks that you believe are your responsibility. This is very common. However, by delegating these tasks you will be able to provide yourself and your family with more and you will be helping to create income for someone else. This will help them to put food on their table while freeing you up to do the things that you love most and the things that are going to help grow your business.

Time Blocking

As far as finding the balance, I would encourage you to schedule ongoing tasks and projects into your calendar and even go as far as color-coding your time blocks. This will enable you to determine which projects or tasks are the most important. It will also assist you in determining your business time, as well as your personal time with family and friends.

To maximize your effectiveness, you may want to actually schedule time for writing and posting to your blog. You can either post daily or weekly, or you can write several posts and schedule them to go live on a specific date in the future. This is a great practice because if something comes up or you go on vacation, you'll still have new and fresh content posting to your blog.

Another essential area to block out is time for creating audio and video, which I highly recommend. This way you will have time scheduled for this task. Here again, you may want to create content that keeps you a few weeks ahead of schedule.

The Six Most Important Things

We all know there is never enough time in the day. If we have systems in place, however, there is much we can accomplish.

When I first started my business, I didn't have a plan. I would go through my day and my week working for hours every day, but it didn't seem like I was accomplishing anything. In the morning I would write a big long to-do list and accomplish fifteen or twenty of the items on the list. Still, I felt as if I had not accomplished anything!

Then I heard this great piece of advice. Each day make a list of the six most important things to accomplish that day. Go about prioritizing those things, check them off, and when completed, you've completed your work for the day. This allows you to prioritize the most important tasks and when you work with focus, you can reward yourself by taking time to also enjoy life. This practice gave me so much freedom! I still had dozens of items on my "to-do" list, but it really helped me prioritize the six most important ones as well as giving me a sense of accomplishment.

I decided that I wanted to maximize my time even further by delegating things that I didn't personally need to be doing. To help me identify these things, I took a piece of paper and divided it into two columns. In one column, on the left-hand side, I listed things that only I could do. Anything that could be delegated, whether I felt that I could do it better or not, I would list in the right hand "to-be-delegated" column. As an exercise, I kept this paper with me for three days, and each time I began a new task, I listed it on one of the columns.

For example, packaging products or preparing mailings could be delegated. Mentoring and training my distributors, writing blog posts, or making phone calls to my best customers could not. You'll find that the activities in your left-hand column have more to do with people, while activities that can be delegated have more to do with paper. What I found a bit embarrassing, but also interesting and quite helpful, was that 75 percent of what I was doing could be delegated to somebody else. Once I began delegating, I was able to accomplish more and my business grew exponentially.

Time Management Tips

Time management is an essential part of building a successful business. When you are building a home-based business, you may have the tendency to go through the day and work on whatever comes across your field of vision while moving from project to project without aim. But there is a better way to manage your day.

- Begin to delegate more. Take a piece of paper and divide it in half. As you go through the week, create a list of all of your activities. Anything that can be delegated, put in one column, anything that is essential for you to attend to, put in the other column. Highlight the top five things you'd like to delegate and then get the help you need.

- Each day compose a "Six Most Important Things to Accomplish" list. This will keep you focused and maximize your results.
- Prioritize people time over paper time (you can delegate paperwork or do it after business hours).
- Let the phone machine pick up incoming calls when you have scheduled something else for that time.
- Limit the number of times you check email each day.

Developing an Online Branding Strategy

The next step in developing your online presence is to develop an online branding strategy. Decide what it is you want to be known as, known for, or what you are going to be selling or offering. The cornerstone of your online business is your blog. Please note that the blog platform has become the new Web site, thus giving the blog owner complete control over design and content. Throughout this book, the word "Web site" is synonymous with the word "blog."

I'll cover blogs and blogging in great detail in the next chapter. The reason I bring it up now is because you will need a domain name (Web address), for your blog (Web site) and this domain name is a huge piece of your online branding jigsaw puzzle. You want to pick a domain name that reflects your branded image, your products, your service, your name, or your program. Pick something that you want to be known for. For example, I know a woman who calls herself "The Card Gal" and I know someone else who calls himself "The Article Guy." They are branding their expertise or their service offering and when they use this nickname, or a close variation, as their username on the social networks, they will be growing their brand.

As you begin to brand yourself on the Internet, keep this fact in mind, and you and your followers will benefit greatly. Give thought to why you want to market your business online and what image you want to convey. Next, determine who your target or niche market is. This will provide you with focus and the ability to brand yourself as an expert in your chosen field.

The next thing you'll want to do is to purchase a .com domain name for your Web site and email addresses. Setting up a branded email address is easy to do and most services provide excellent tutorials and/or customer support to assist you. This will give you a professional presence and you can include this information on your business cards. In selecting a domain name, choose something that is easy to say, spell, and remember. Additionally, choose a name that identifies what it is that you offer.

Here is an analogy between your storefront business and your online business. Your store's name and street address are analogous to your domain name. If someone wants to come to your store, they need to have your store name and your address so that they can find you. Your domain serves as both your store sign and your street address. This is the URL that people will type in the address bar of their Web browser to find your Web site. It is important for people to have an idea as to what your site is about based on your domain name; this will also help with search engine optimization and better ranking in Google.

Setting Up Shop	
Brick and Mortar Business	**Online Business**
Store Name and Street Address	Domain Name
The Land	Hosting Service
The Building	Blog or Web site
News Ads and Yellow Pages	Web Ads, Articles, Forums
Radio or Television Ads	Audio and Video Marketing
Networking Groups	Social Networking

Once you have your domain name, you will want to secure your Web hosting. Your Web hosting is comparable to the land where you build your store. It is your online real estate where you house your Web site.

The hosting service I recommend is Host Gator (www.WebHostingGator.com) which allows you to have a lot of control over your Web site. It is also extremely economical because you can host unlimited domains on one Host Gator account. As far as where to go to purchase your domain name,

GoDaddy (www.BestDomainPricing.com) is an excellent choice, as you have access to all of your domain names from one control panel.

The foundation of your Internet empire is your Web site. This is your online storefront or office building. Your Web site is where you can house your content, build a community, make sales, and grow your business. It is crucial that your Web site reflect your branded image and that you provide ways for people to get to know you.

- Have a welcome audio or video message that your visitors can click on.
- Display written, audio, or video testimonials from your customers and students.
- Make sure your Web site is a warm and inviting place where people will want to frequent.
- Post fresh and informative content.

Continuing the analogy, let's talk about advertising. Perhaps you advertise your storefront business on the radio or in your local newspaper. Online you can advertise on Google, Facebook, or by purchasing ad space on someone's Web site. There are also numerous ways that you can advertise your business for free. You can place your signature, business name, tagline and Web address in your signature on the social networks or forums. You can write articles and in the bio box at the end of each article you can invite people to visit your Web site. You can also advertise via a YouTube video, linking viewers to your products. I will cover this in detail later.

Networking and interacting with others is a vital component of relationship marketing. Regarding networking, in your community you can go to the Chamber of Commerce or business networking groups; online, we have social networks and forums. Social networks and forums are to your online business what offline business groups are to more traditional brick and mortar businesses. So, as you can see, setting up an online business is much like setting up and promoting an offline business.

Action Steps

Here are seven steps that you can take to put what you've learned into action.

1. Schedule time to develop your online presence.
2. Create a list of items that require your prioritized attention.
3. Create a list of projects and tasks that can be delegated.
4. Identify your branded colors and image.
5. Select a .com domain that reflects your brand, program or product.
6. Set up your branded email address.
7. Create branded business cards.

Resources Mentioned in This Chapter

Host Gator: www.WebHostingGator.com
Go Daddy: www.BestDomainPricing.com

Blogging: The Hub of Your Online Empire

Your blog is not just where people go for content; it's where they go to connect with you. With your blog, you build community, you build credibility, and you create interaction. Your blog can house your audios, your videos, and your articles. Your blog can also serve as a membership site, your online store and your Web radio or TV show!

Blogging is a big, exciting, and mysterious subject, one that I hope to shine the light on for you. Today's blog is also considered to be the new Web site, allowing you to easily have complete access to and control of your site along with a Web presence where people can learn about you, your interests, and your expertise.

What is a Blog?

Traditionally, a blog is a contraction of "Web log". It is similar to an online diary where a person can go and post his or her thoughts and get people to comment and create conversations. But today's blog is much, much more than that, and most Internet marketers use the blog platform as their Web site. It is still called the blog because it is housed, for example, on the WordPress platform.

A blog creates a platform from which you can speak, positioning you as an expert in your field. Your blog is a place where you can showcase products, share your thoughts, and build community. If you are part of a team or company or you are taking an online course, you might want to have a blog so you have a central location with easy access to training materials. If you are passionate about baking and you want to share that passion with others, you can put your recipes or sneak-peeks of recipes on your blog, thus encouraging people to buy your book.

Here are several examples of how a blog might be used.

- A membership site
- A training center
- A community center
- A list-building platform to collect potential clients' names

- A Web TV show
- An online radio show
- A marketplace
- A showcase for featured products

A Blog versus Traditional Web Site

Traditional Web sites require a high level of expertise and knowledge of HTML (Hypertext Markup Language) coding. They typically require a significant financial investment and when anything needs to be changed, you'll need to pay your Web designer to make the changes for you. Unlike a traditional Web site, a blog allows you to have complete control over your content without having to pay a Web developer.

A WordPress blog looks very much like a traditional Web site, but it is very user friendly and it's a snap to add or change content. You simply click a button to get into the dashboard area where you are able to post an article, change a picture, or add an audio or a video as easily as it would be to create something in a Word document. It really is that easy and it gives you a lot of flexibility. Whenever you want to make a change to your blog, just log in, make the changes, click save, and the changes are instantly active on the site.

The other major reason to use the blog platform, aside from the ease of use and control you have of your site, is that search engines love blogs. With the blog platform you are adding content on a regular basis, and that is what search engines look for: fresh new content for their audience.

To establish your blog as an authority site and to keep your viewers coming back regularly, it is recommended that you post new content at least once a week, ideally even more often.

You can encourage your readers to comment on your blog posts and begin an online conversation with them. You can also send out a tweet on Twitter and let people know that you just posted an article on a given topic and that you'd value their feedback. Include a link to the actual post and that will drive more traffic to your site.

You can set your blog up so that when people arrive at your site, they will either land on a page that has your newest posts on a variety of topics or you can create what they call a static page, which gives it more of a traditional Web site look that is not constantly changing. By creating a static page, your posts won't show up on the main page but they will show up on a page that you designate as the blog page.

Your home page can have written content, images, or even a video. You ultimately want it to be an inviting place so that your viewers want to stay and explore.

Free versus Premium Blogging Platforms

The most effective and powerful blog platform is WordPress.org (www.WordPress.org), where you can set up a self-hosted blog; giving you ownership of the domain and the online real estate. There are free blog platforms such as Blogger (www.Blogger.com)

and WordPress.com (www.WordPress.com) but there are several disadvantages to having your blog on a free platform. First of all, you don't own the online real estate or domain name, which means that at any point the hosting site could disable your account. Additionally, the free blog platforms post links on your site to entice your readers to click over to view someone else's content.

Here's an analogy that might clarify this. Having a blog on a free platform is like renting an apartment. Having a self-hosted blog is like owning your own home. Another benefit to having a self-hosted blog is that you will rank much higher in the search engines.

The Top Four Reasons to Host Your Blog on Your Own Domain

In order to be seen as a serious Internet marketer or serious online businessperson it is wise to invest in a domain name and self-host your Web site/blog.

1. Having a blog hosted on your own domain gives you the liberty to make necessary changes or additions as often as you see fit. This will enable you to keep your brand consistent with all your other sites or work online.
2. Hosting your Web site or blog on your own domain will make it easier for people to remember your name and brand. Search engine optimization (SEO) is essential to your success online and the recognition of your

brand. Using the correct keywords for your site will increase traffic to your blog, which is your ultimate goal. You can use keywords in your domain name as well as in the titles of your blog posts and the search engines will take note.

3. Self-hosting provides added security as well as easy access to your site.
4. Self-hosting ultimately provides a more professional appearance when compared to many of the other Web sites and blogs on the Internet.

Based on the advantages outlined above, if you are serious about your online business, you must consider hosting your blog on your own domain.

Setting up your blog is very easy to do. You can either pay someone to set your blog up for you or you may prefer to go through a series of video tutorials and set your blog up yourself. Blogging is huge for building your community. You are also building your list, sharing your thoughts, encouraging interaction, and sharing your audios and your videos.

Blogs are a great way to build a relationship with your readers. Your blog houses every aspect of your online business. It's your storefront, shopping cart, community center, information center, classroom, and more.

Because your blog is such an essential component and the hub of your online world, I am offering a free companion course which will provide you with an in-depth understanding and practical application of blogging. You can find details at the back of the book.

The Anatomy of a Blog

Okay, now that you know what a blog is, let's talk a bit about the various blog components. One of the most common questions I hear is "What is the difference between a blog post and a blog page?" Another component of a blog that seems to mystify people is the use of plugins. Let me shed some light on these aspects of a blog so that you can gain a better understanding and become better equipped to begin posting articles and using plugins on your own blog.

Post versus Page

Let's talk now about the difference between a "post" and a "page." A post is an article that shows up on your blog page along with other posts. You may have noticed that when content is posted to a blog, the most current post is at the top of the page and older posts move down the page over time. Let's say you write on the topic of natural health and you want to post a variety of articles over the course of weeks or months. You can have all of those articles labeled with a category called natural health. Every time you create a new post and you click that it belongs to the category of natural health, it is going to show up on the post page and it is also going to show up when your readers click on the category link to "natural health," along with all the other posts on that topic.

A page is different from a post because a page is static, meaning that the content does not change every time you create a blog post. The content on your pages only changes when you intentionally add or remove content. A page on a blog is similar to a traditional Web site page.

The exception to this is the blog page. This is the page where your blog posts will be displayed. On the blog page, you will typically see a mini synopsis and an image, for each post. You can click to view the full article or you can scroll down the page to look at other blog post topics. If you want to read more on any post, you can click to access the full article.

That in a nutshell is the essential difference between a post and a page. Posts can be assigned to a category or belong to more than one category. A page is more like your traditional Web site page where you have more control over what is displayed and where on the page it is displayed.

WordPress Plugins

Plugins are tools that extend the functionality of your site. Most plugins are free, but be selective in your use of plugins. There are thousands upon thousands to choose from, and they will slow down your site if you add too many. If you are interested in finding out more about WordPress plugins, you can either visit www.WordPress.org/extend or you can visit Powerful Plugins (www.PowerfulPlugins.com).

Adding an Opt-In Box to Your Blog

A very effective way to grow your business and your relationships with your readers is to have a way for them to sign up (opt-in) to your email list. You want to do this carefully and strategically, because most people are overwhelmed with the quantity of email they receive each day. You can offer your readers an audio recording of an interview with someone they would be interested in hearing about, or a report or eBook on a topic of interest.

AWeber (www.WebmailConnections.com) is considered to be the best email marketing company on the Internet. Your account with them includes the ability to set up an unlimited number of lists, create online newsletters, broadcast your blog posts, and set up an attractive lead capture opt-in box on your blog. When people type in their name and email address, they will automatically receive an email, delivering what you offered. You must be sure to set up your email marketing list to include the automation of sending out a message when someone opts in to your list. This is very easy to set up and there are very clear instructions on the AWeber site along with an excellent customer support staff.

1ShoppingCart (www.BestShoppingCartSystem.com) is another highly recommended service that provides you with unlimited auto responders along with a shopping cart and an affiliate program. Having a shopping cart allows you to be able to easily sell from your site. Having an affiliate program provides you with a system for encouraging people to refer your products

35

and programs in exchange for an affiliate commission. When people purchase through your affiliate's link, 1ShoppingCart will track the sales and the commissions.

They have a 30-day trial that provides you with full access to the system, if this is something you want to explore. Dr. Jeanette Cates has also developed a step-by-step training program (www.YourOneHourShoppingCart.com) to get you up and running quickly. I took this program and highly recommend it. Jeanette is an exceptional educator and highly successful Internet marketer.

Automating Your Blog Posts and Generating Content

You have the option of having your posts go live immediately, or you can schedule them to publish on a specific date. You may prefer to write several articles at a time and schedule them to appear over the course of the week, month, or year. This is also a task you can delegate. Theoretically, you could assign fifty-two articles to be scheduled to post on your blog once a week. Fifty-two articles may sound like a lot of content but it really isn't a lot if you use the transcripts from an hour-long seminar that you deliver.

I also recommend that you schedule time in your calendar for writing. By doing this you will create a positive habit and you will get your message out and create a lot of content.

Adding Content to Your Blog

It is very easy to add content to your blog. Once you log in to your blog, open up a new post and begin to type. It's as easy as that. You will see two tabs to the right of the posting area that say "visual" or "HTML." It you want to add written content and format the content, you click on the "visual" tab. If you are going to be adding HTML, for example from a YouTube video embed code, you will see at the top right of your blog post, a tab that says HTML. That is telling your post that you are adding code. Once you publish or update your post, this code enables your viewers to see your YouTube video.

A post can be a paragraph or two long or the equivalent of a page or two in length. Some bloggers prefer longer articles (posts), while others feel that if their posts are longer than a few paragraphs, the average person won't make it all the way through the article. If your article is a manageable length and you use white space, colorful images, and space between your thoughts, people are more likely to read your posts. The more informative, user-friendly, and reader-friendly your posts are, the more often people are going to come back to your site.

Creating Content

It is not uncommon for people to wonder what they would write about. You can write about your passions, interests, or what you are knowledgeable about. You can write your reactions to a news story, recount an experience you've had, or share your opinion on any given topic. The first step to becoming a prolific blogger is to schedule a time to write each day. The more you write, the more your ideas will flow. I've found it helpful to map out my blog posts each month or each season. One of my favorites is the "Ten Tips" format. Decide on a theme and then list ten things that you know about that theme. Those then become the titles for your "Ten Tips."

Expert Content for Your Blog

Post articles from well-known experts in your field. You can find an unlimited amount of this type of content on Ezine Articles (www.EzineArticles.com). Be sure to read their agreement policy, though, as you are entitled to post a limited number of articles each year.

Another way to get expert content is from YouTube. Video blogging is very popular and, if you research carefully, you can find high-quality video content that your readers will love. Using YouTube videos is a great place to start as you begin to develop your own videos. We'll discuss video creation more in depth in Chapter Seven.

Another way to get fantastic content for your blog is to post audio interviews and excerpts of the transcripts of these interviews. By interviewing thought leaders in your field and posting that content on your blog, you can quickly become known as an industry expert and go-to person yourself!

Guest Bloggers

A very popular method for generating content for your blog is to have guest bloggers. Guest blogging is when someone posts articles to your blog or you post articles on other blogs. You can do this formally or informally. The most effective way to gain value from guest blogging is to strategically post on blogs that have a readership that includes your target audience and to have guest bloggers on your blog who can offer content that your readership would enjoy and benefit from. Internet marketer Nicole Dean developed an actual system that is based on guest blogging. You can read about it on the Blog World Tour Web site (www.BlogWorldTour.com). Consider having guest bloggers on your blog. It is a lot of fun and adds a lot of value!

Color and Branding

As you design your blog, incorporate your branded colors or give thought to what colors and images best portray the message you want to convey to your audience. If your target market is motorcycle riders, the look of your blog is going to be very different than if your market is corporate executives. You want to consider your audience as well as your personality when you create the image of your site. An industry favorite source for WordPress themes is the Studio Press Themes Web site (www.ThemesbyStudioPress.com). They have a wide variety of color and design options to choose from and they offer exceptional customer support in their user forum.

Common Blog Mistake

One of the most common mistakes people make with blogging is to try to sell to people right away. You don't want to sell them stuff; you want to sell them on you. You want to have them eager to hear from you and appreciative of the information you provide. While your readers are going to want to buy from you, don't try to sell, especially while you are trying to build that relationship.

Posting Video to Your Blog

The easiest way to add video to your site is by adding a YouTube video. You just go over to YouTube, get the embed code from your video or a video that you'd like to feature, and pop it into the HTML tab of a new post or page. There are specific plugins that allow you to do more advanced things with video. The only thing about using a YouTube video is that when people double click on a video that is posted on your site, it will take them straight to YouTube and off of your site. The way to avoid this is to create your own videos that you host on your own site or an independent server. We'll go into these things in more detail in Chapter Seven.

Getting People to Visit Your Site Often

One of the easiest ways to get people to come to your site often is to post part of an article in your online newsletter or email marketing pieces and invite your readers to visit your site to read the rest of the article. You could also create video articles and invite your readers to view these on your site.

Blog as Membership Site

Incorporating a membership component to your blog is a great way to build community and deepen relationships with your readers and target market. When you add a membership component to your blog you, in essence, create an online classroom, portal, or community center. You can have a variety of membership levels, including a free membership level. The premier WordPress membership plugin is Wishlist Membership Plugin (www.WishlistMembershipPlugin.com).

If you are interested in a membership site, you may want to review the Wishlist Membership Plugin. They have a guaranteed trial period, exceptional customer support, and more than twenty step-by-step video tutorials. Additionally, Dr. Jeanette Cates has developed a training program to help you get up to speed quickly at her Web site (www.YourOneHourMembershipSite.com).

Income that you receive from online membership payments is called "continuity income." I've seen membership sites priced anywhere between $7.95 and $997.00 per month. You do the math!

In your membership area you can provide:

- Product downloads
- Access to course material

- Information about members-only Webinars
- Special bonuses

Having a membership site will position you as an authority in your niche. It will also build a loyal following and stream of ongoing income and referrals (as your members recommend your site to others).

Stu McLaren, co-owner of Wishlist Membership Plugin has a great quote on this topic. He says, "People come for the content, but stay for the community." You want to provide your members with valuable content and you want to provide them with a way to interact with the other members. Interactive member-only webinars are one way to accomplish this; a members-only forum is another great way to provide your members with a way to interact with one another. There is even a WordPress plugin called Simple Press Forum (www.SimplePressForum.com) that will allow you to create a forum right inside of your WordPress blog.

Membership sites provide:

- A "home" for your following
- A great way for people to get to know you
- A way for you to become known as an expert in your field
- A loyal following
- Value to your members
- Easy access to your products and programs
- A way to funnel students into your next-level programs

- A fantastic way to generate an ongoing income stream
- A vehicle for creating new products and programs based on the needs of your members
- A way to create an affiliate program and multiply your results

Building Up Your Membership

Offer a free level of membership or the opportunity for people to subscribe to your free digital newsletter. Too many sites focus on trying to get a paying member as their primary goal. Instead focus on encouraging them to subscribe for your free digital newsletter list and begin to build a relationship with them. In this way you will have a much stronger chance of having them become a part of your community.

Action Steps

Here are seven steps that you can take to put what you've learned into action.

1. Purchase your domain name.
2. Establish a hosting account.
3. Setup your WordPress blog.
4. Select a blog theme that reflects your brand.
5. Create blog posts and blog pages.
6. Ad an opt-in box to your blog's sidebar and create your first auto responder message.
7. Schedule time to write posts weekly and invite comments and conversations.

Resources Mentioned in This Chapter

Host Gator: www.WebHostingGator.com
Go Daddy: www.BestDomainPricing.com
1ShoppingCart: www.BestShoppingCartSystem.com
One Hour Shopping Cart:
    www.YourOneHourShoppingCart.com
One Hour Membership Site:
    www.YourOneHourMembershipSite.com
AWeber: www.WebmailConnections.com
StudioPress: www.ThemesbyStudioPress.com
Wishlist: www.WishlistMembershipPlugin.com
Powerful Plugins: www.PowerfulPlugins.com
Ezine Articles: www.EzineArticles.com
Simple Press: www.SimplePressForum.com
Blog World Tour: www.BlogWorldTour.com

Social Networking
Strategies and Techniques

Networking online is much like networking offline. You need to find effective ways to connect with people and bring value to them, and thus begin to build a relationship with them. Social networking is a powerful way to grow your network, your brand recognition and your business. There are hundreds of social networks on the Internet today. We are going to discuss the "Big Three": Twitter, Facebook, and LinkedIn. We'll also discuss ways to maximize your time with social networking along with specific tips and strategies that you can put into play immediately.

45

Social networking, just like in-person networking, is about building relationships, not selling your products or services to people. Instead, sell them on "you" and create raving fans. As an example, think about messages you get on social networks. Which are the ones you read and which are the ones you delete? How do you feel about the person who is always trying to sell you something?

Relationship marketing is about building relationships with people both online and offline. It's caring about people, helping people, answering questions, building relationships, making referrals, and asking for referrals. These are essential steps in getting closer to people. Once you've built trust with someone, it's easy to get introduced to their network. Then when their friends thank them for introducing them to you, it's going to reflect positively on the person who made the introduction!

In today's competitive environment, how can you stay ahead of the competition, brand yourself as a true expert in your field and provide a way for your audience to come to know, like, and trust you? The answer is via social networking.

An essential social networking strategy is to take the time to set up your social networking profiles on Twitter, Facebook, and LinkedIn. You want to portray a professional presence, share your interests and accomplishments, and list references and testimonials. Once you have your profile set up, spend some time exploring each site. Use the same photo on each site so that you develop a branded image across the social networks. A professional-looking, attractive headshot is what you'll want. Invest in a new photo if yours is outdated or if you don't have a professional quality image. However, be sure to choose a photo that reflects your personality and that will attract individuals you will want to connect with.

Tips to Enhance Your Social Networking Profiles and Experience

- Create a professional-looking profile.
- Add a professional-looking headshot photo of yourself. Make sure to select a photo where you are smiling as this makes a positive impact and draws people to you.
- Schedule fifteen minutes a day or thirty to sixty minutes a week to interact on your social networks.
- Join a few groups on topics of interest to you.
- Participate in group discussions: ask and answer questions.
- Set up your signature to include your Web address and tagline.
- Consider setting your email preferences so that the bulk of the messages from your social networks stay on the network and are not sent to your email box; this will let you focus on these messages when you have scheduled social networking time.
- Sell them **on you,** not on your business; build relationships and be of help to others.

Participating in groups and on forums that attract your niche market is an effective way to build relationships and grow your business. A word of caution: just as in the real world, you want to use common sense and good judgment. Most social networks allow you to email back and forth from within the system and thus you do not need to give out your personal information unless you want to.

Grow a Social Networking Presence

You can grow a vibrant social networking presence in as little as fifteen minutes per day. The trick is to schedule this time in your calendar. This way you'll stay focused and you'll prioritize your social networking time. Here are a few activities to choose from:

- Visit your social networks.
- Check your messages.
- Post a status update, sharing something about you, or something that you are working on, in a way that will create interest and not in a way that sounds like a sales pitch.
- Visit one or more of your groups and comment on discussions.
- Begin a discussion topic and encourage others to chime in.

I've found that I get the most responses when I share something interesting but not too personal. For example, when I've shared about a great book I read or course that I took, people comment back and join in the conversation. I also find that when I share something humorous I get the most responses.

As an example, I came across a (fictitious) video that featured an application for a cell phone that translates animal languages. On Facebook, I got many comments from people thanking me for the chuckle or commenting on ideas for other clever gadgets. Now those people are having conversations with each other based on what they were talking about. This type of information is a conversation starter and something that makes people smile.

Finding ways to connect with people and share something of value or interest with them will help to bridge the gap. Social networking is perfect for accomplishing this. Be sure to keep in mind that building trust and building relationships online takes time. You don't want to become known as someone who is always trying to sell something. Instead, become known as a person who has a lot of knowledge and experience to offer.

You can accomplish this via social networking by participating in group discussions and helping others. People will become accustomed to seeing your name, and, in many cases, your photograph. You can also initiate conversations by asking questions. Frame your questions in ways that encourages people to reply. For example, which question would you be more inclined to answer? 1) "I have a great product that can help you save a lot of money, so buy my stuff!" or 2) "I noticed last week that Jim K. was asking for suggestions on how to connect with health professionals in Canada. I posted a few ideas, which I hope he found helpful. Today I'd appreciate your tips on how I can connect with massage therapists in New England."

A great way to drive traffic to your blog or Web site is by having your Web address in your profile signature. This is viewed as an acceptable and low-key way to market your business and also provides people with a way to find out more about each other's products and services. Once you know your way around, you may want to initiate a group discussion. This will shine the light on you and will facilitate relationship building and the possibility of future business and referrals. Become known as an expert in your field. Set yourself apart by adding audio and video to your social networking profiles and at least once a week post a reply to a question or participate in a discussion.

Facebook Tips

Once again, be sure to use a professional photograph for your profile. Set up a fan page and brand it with your image or logo. Take care to name your page as an extension of your brand.

Facebook allows you to create a customized page for your fans to "like." You can include pictures, text-links, videos, and many other pertinent applications. To create a customized landing page, search through the Facebook applications and find the Facebook Markup Language (FBML) application. FBML is Facebook's version of HTML (Hypertext Markup Language). The FBML application allows you to place limited aspects of HTML coding onto your Facebook page, thus allowing you to format the color, size and style of font as well as being able to add code for images. This will allow you to customize your Facebook page.

You can also import your blog feed to Facebook so that every time you post to your blog, your fan page is automatically updated. Of course, fans are then able to read and comment on your blog post directly on your fan page.

One of my favorite Facebook applications is Networked Blogs (www.NetworkedBlogs.com). This application allows you to place a widget on your blog as a way of adding followers to your Networked Blogs feed. Once you have twenty followers, Facebook will syndicate your blog content.

It's vital that you interact with your fans. We are in the midst of a marketing revolution that revolves around building and sustaining relationships. Therefore, it's vital that you participate in the discussion, answer questions, and take the time to engage with your fans on a daily basis.

Your Facebook fan page is no different than other social media platforms. You can promote your events, share engaging content with your readers, and, through regular status updates, share interesting facts about your industry. You can also integrate your blog posts and publish informative videos and articles that will position you as an expert within your industry.

LinkedIn Tips

The LinkedIn social network is another essential component to your social networking strategy. On LinkedIn, you have the ability to share a great deal of information about yourself, including your background, accomplishments, education, and much more. You can, in essence, set up an online resume on LinkedIn. I have personally been contacted by people wanting to do business with me as a result of the professional quality of my LinkedIn profile.

LinkedIn has a wide variety of interest groups that you can participate in. The best strategy is to join fewer groups in order to participate more often. You may also choose to start a group, which is a great way to market your name and brand. Consider creating a buzz around the topics of conversation that your target market and you are interested in.

Search and find the groups that either you are interested in or your target market will be involved in, and join those in order to position your name and brand for more exposure.

LinkedIn gives you the opportunity to add different applications to your profile page, such as videos or PowerPoint presentations. There is also a way to ask for testimonials from your contacts, which will be made public to those who visit your profile page. The main purpose of LinkedIn and any other social network is to build connections and ultimately relationships. Each network has a different platform and method of approaching this, but all are great avenues to build your brand and name.

Get involved in discussions and people will take note. Be a giver, offer ideas and suggestions and make introductions when you are able to.

Twitter Tips

Twitter is a social network that provides a platform to communicate your 140 character messages— known as tweets—to the world. It is considered a micro-blog, as you are constantly adding new content. The restriction of using only 140 characters enables you to be unique with your message. Some may find this aspect challenging, but when you are able to perfect it to a point where you are not sounding like a salesperson then your audience will grow.

Begin by customizing your profile page. Select a user name that identifies you or relates to your business. The next step is to click on the settings tab and customize your profile and preferences. Be sure to list your Web or blog address so that anyone who goes to your Twitter page can quickly access your site. You'll also want to add a description about your business and upload your photo. Next choose one of several background themes or upload a custom theme, thus setting you apart and creating interest. You can choose to have notices sent to your email address or not. In today's busy world, with so much email, you may elect not to receive notices via email but rather make a point of checking them when you login to your Twitter account.

Once you have your account set up, you'll want to begin following and getting followers. One thing you can do is search any online mail services that you use, such as Gmail and Yahoo!, to see whether anyone in your address book has already registered an account on Twitter. From that same screen, you can send out an invitation to anyone in your address book to join you on Twitter.

There are a couple of ways to get followers. One is to add a badge or widget on your blog or Web site inviting people to follow you on Twitter. Another way to gain followers is to find other Twitter accounts within your niche by searching keywords on Twitter or at search.twitter.com. Follow the people who are following them. Many of those people will follow you back.

Now that you have followers, you can begin tweeting messages. In addition to inviting people to stop by your blog or Web site, consider tweeting links to interesting articles or sites that you've discovered. Make sure that your tweets are of value or people will un-follow you just as fast as they followed you, because no one wants to receive numerous "buy my stuff" messages.

Relationship Marketing with Social Networking

How do you make your online social networking relationships some of the best ones you have? Follow discussions and get to know people who are writing on topics that are of interest to you. If people capture your attention, go to their profile pages and click on the link to visit their Web sites. In that way you can find out more about them and their business. This will also provide you with information in case you are inspired to start up a conversation with them.

I have established several very important business connections in this way. The beauty of these types of relationships is that the connection usually happens because people genuinely like and/or admire one another. In the online community, it is not unusual to team up on projects or create joint venture partnerships.

Blitz Time (www.BlitzTime.com) is another social networking site that offers a unique way to network. Members meet via a phone conferencing service for training and networking. In addition to participating in training sessions and group conversations, their phone technology allows members to meet one-on-one. I've used this service as a way to deliver training, meet with my team and network with other professionals.

One of my favorite Twitter tools is called Hoot Suite (www.HootSuite.com). This is an online program that allows you to set up columns of Twitter users based on criteria that you establish. For example, one column can be for any mentions using your Twitter ID. Another column can be for your direct messages. You can also set up columns for specific hashtags and group names. Since I began using Hoot Suite, my online relationships have grown and the number of subscribers to my blog has multiplied.

If you would like to learn more about social networking and social media marketing, you may want to refer to Connie Ragen Green's course on the topic. (www.SocialNetworksToday.com). Connie is an exceptional educator who teaches in a way that makes it easy to learn and retain information.

Get Involved in Conversations

When you login to Facebook or LinkedIn you can see the update feed for people in your network and you also get to see whom they're interacting with and what groups they are participating in. The best way to grow relationships is to become known as a giver. Take time to answer questions in your area of expertise. This is going to show that you are a giving person as well as a knowledgeable person. When it comes across that you care more about people than you do about their money, people will take note.

On LinkedIn you can ask questions of the community. If you ask a question that's clearly a sales pitch, people are going to disregard you or think poorly of you. At the same time, if you ask a thought provoking question, people will respond. I have a story about this. My company had recently expanded into Australia. I was looking for ideas on how to connect with professionals in that country and thus decided to reach out to the LinkedIn community. I carefully worded my question by sharing that, "our company has expanded into Australia. I would really value your input as I'm looking for ideas on how I can connect with professionals in Australia." I didn't say, "Do you live in Australia? I can help you grow your business." I reached out for help.

I received 35 responses in 24 hours. I was amazed and appreciative. I wrote to one person and said "I so appreciate your suggestion. I'd like to ask you a question, though. Why did you take the time to answer me?" They provided me with a very thorough answer and many of the other responses included personal introductions to individuals or to organizations. The response I received was, "Oh, that's easy. I always see you on the networks answering other people's' questions. I was glad to help." So in social networking it is key to be respectful of people as well as to participate in conversations, questions and interest groups.

Tips for Harnessing the Power of Social Networking to Grow Your Business

Once you have developed a presence on the social networking platforms with your name, brand, and Web site information as well as your picture, you will begin to get noticed for your expertise provided—of course—that you have shared information and joined along in conversations with others. Remember, the key to building relationships and communities is giving of yourself with no expectation of getting anything in return. This simple concept will set you apart from the rest and ultimately get you noticed. And now let's turn to another aspect of growing your overall network: establishing an in-person network.

Ten Tips for Maximizing Your Effectiveness with In-Person Networking

To develop a well-rounded networking strategy, you will want to participate in in-person networking. In-person networking allows you the opportunity to be able to quickly connect with people. Let's explore a few effective strategies for developing your "know, like, and trust" factor through in-person networking.

1. Arrive early and stay late

Arriving early allows you to connect with the organizers, the movers and shakers, and greet people as they come through the door. You become familiar to them, because if you do this over time, you will become a known entity and a familiar face to people. You will also be able to build relationships by helping others build relationships. As people arrive, since you know who is already there, you can help make introductions. Let's say that a graphic designer walks through the door and you know that there is Web designer in the room who was just talking about needing to have a logo designed for a client. You could easily make that introduction which could turn into a good alliance and both of these people will be grateful to you for having made this connection.

The reason to stay late is that you'll get to network with the people who stay late. You'll also become known to the Chamber of Commerce officers or the hosting organization as a person who gives and a person who can be counted on to be there and to help. In time, they may want to feature you in their newsletter, ask you to serve on a committee, or even have you as a guest speaker, which will put you in front of even more people. You become known as a go-to person, a person who networks, and a person who is serious about their business.

2. Mingle, reach out, and circulate

When you attend networking events, focus on networking, mingling, and getting to know people. What you don't want to do is spend the bulk of the time sitting and chatting with the people that you work with. If you arrive at the event with colleagues, make a plan with them to get to know new people and compare notes afterwards. You are there to network and meet other people. If you find yourself squirreled up in the corner with people whom you know, find a way to extract yourself so that you can mingle and meet new people.

When you are networking with new people there are a few things to consider. It is better to connect with fewer people and go deeper than it is to connect with more people on a surface level.

If you find yourself speaking with someone and there seems to be a good connection and you get a sense that continuing the conversation would be a good use of time, spend more time with that person. However, you don't want to keep him or her from connecting with other people. You may want to check in with this new contact to see if he or she would like to continue the conversation or would prefer to circulate and perhaps get together for lunch or coffee later in the week. At that time you can take the relationship to the next level.

If you are in a group of two or three people and they are gossiping or speaking negatively or for whatever reason you don't feel there is good synergy, find a reason to extract yourself. You can simply say, "I've enjoyed our conversation. I'm going to go mingle; let's connect up later." Then just politely remove yourself and find another group to connect with.

3. Listen more than you speak

When you connect with someone, you don't want to start the conversation telling them all about you and your products and then give them your card and tell them to visit your Web site. That person will throw your card away. Instead, when you connect with people, ask them to tell you about themselves. You can ask questions like: "So, tell me about your business. Have you been in town a long time? Aside from business, what do you enjoy doing? If you could do anything with your time, what would you do?" Find out about them because you might be able to make a connection for them. If, for example, they tell you that they love boating or skydiving and you know someone on the other side of the room that shares the same passion, you can make a wonderful introduction. Then you'll become known as a connector and this will be another way for you to add value. This will also deepen your relationships with these people because they will realize that you are not all about business but that you are also very committed to building relationships. Increase your likeability factor and become known as a person of value before you try to "get" business from your network. It's more important to sell your network on you than on your product.

4. Bring business cards with you to events

There are a number of fabulous and affordable printing services, such as VistaPrint (www.VistaPrint.com), where you can design your business cards online. But be careful of the free business card offer, even though that might be tempting. Some of the free services will imprint their company name on the reverse side of your card. What kind of image will this portray if someone flips over your business card and sees this? This might make it seem that you are not a viable business, that you are not successful, or worse yet, that you are too cheap to make the small investment to purchase business cards for your company. Be sure this is not the price you are paying to have free cards.

Spend the money and get yourself a nice set of professional-looking business cards. You may want to put some text on the back of the card such as a quote or a call to action; however I do recommend leaving at least some white space on the back of the card so that people can take notes and thus remember more about you. This is why I further suggest that you do not laminate the back of your cards. Two-sided laminated cards are very difficult to write on. Just opt for the glossy finish on the printed front side.

Let's talk about what you would write on the back of the business cards of the people you are meeting. One thing that I always ask is when their birthday is, as I like to send out birthday cards. Another thing that you can do is, when you are done speaking with them, jot down notes based on your conversation.

You can make note of any comments they made about their business, their contacts, their hobbies, or their family. The more time you spend with fewer people, the more you are going to remember about each person.

Let's say that you collect twenty business cards at an event; you are not going to remember all of those people. This is also a reason to collect the cards of only the people you personally met with versus going over to the materials table and picking up the business card of everyone who attended the event. The exception would be if you pick up a few cards of people you'd like to be introduced to or who have a business that you'd like to find out more about. What you don't want to do is add people to your email list or start to market to them without their permission.

The other thing about business cards is, you don't want to be known as the person who sows business cards as you walk around the room, interrupting groups of people, randomly handing people your business card without stopping to speak with them. Those cards will go into the garbage can. You are better off collecting cards from the people you speak with and spending time connecting with them. This is where the "less is more" theory comes into play, as you don't want to just collect pieces of paper and try to follow up with people you haven't built a relationship with.

It's a good practice to have your Web site, contact number, and email address clearly listed on your card. For networking events, it is an excellent idea to have your photo on your card. When people get home and go through the business cards they've collected, you want them to remember you. Having your photo on your card facilitates this and will make it easier for people to remember who you are.

5. Bring friends, colleagues, and networking buddies with you to events and introduce them to others

Take someone from your BNI chapter to your Chamber of Commerce meeting and introduce them to someone in their contact sphere or introduce them to people whom you feel would be a good connection for them. This will again increase your value and your likeability factor as well as make you an invaluable member of the business community. You will also be helping people at the Chamber of Commerce event to broaden their contact sphere as you help to connect them to people in your BNI chapter.

Bring your networking buddies with you to events but don't hang out with them the whole time. Visit with them, introduce them to people, and then go and mingle. Encourage them to do the same.

6. Make warm introductions to people who are at the event

If you are speaking with a professional organizer and you know that her best referral source is realtors, you may want to introduce her to one or more of the realtors in the room. A possible introduction could go like this, "Lisa, hi, I know that you are a realtor specializing in selling homes in this area. I'd like to introduce you to my good friend Donna. Donna is a professional organizer and she specializes in helping to increase the value of homes with her home staging services. I thought that the two of you might enjoy meeting one another for a possible mutually beneficial relationship." This can increase the services that the realtor offers to her clients and this can create a great alliance between these two professionals.

Again, you increase your value and what you offer to the community and you are deepening your relationships. As an additional benefit to you, you will become more easily referable as you will be on their radar and thus you'll be able to grow your business.

7. Develop a short elevator speech

Rather than saying, "Hi, my name is so-and-so and this is the name of my business and I do this, that, and the other thing and we have great stuff and you should go to our Web site and buy our stuff," you would benefit by developing a captivating elevator speech. This is another situation where the "less is more" factor comes into play. Rather than telling them everything that you do, share with them something that causes them to say, "Tell me more."

I'd like to share a story with you told to me by my very good friend Sasha. She was at a luncheon for financial planners and, being the conversationalist that she is, she turned to the person to her right and asked, "What do you do?" That person went on to tell her all about their financial planning services in great detail. Next, Sasha turned to her left and asked, "what do you do?" This person said, "I show people how to get their children to buy them an island".

Which person would you be more inclined to ask to tell you more? So, what can you say to get people to ask you to tell them more? You may want to practice on a few friends and let them know that you are working on your thirty-second commercial and that your goal is to get people to ask you to tell them more. Ask them if they would listen to what you've come up with and then give you their honest feedback.

8. Get together with people over the course of the month

Select two or three people that you'd like to get to know better and schedule a time to meet with them over the next few weeks. It's a best practice to meet with at least one person a week, outside of networking events. Some people make it a practice to meet with several people a week for coffee or over lunch.

People may not have their calendar with them, so set a tentative date and find out the best way to reach them to confirm that you both have the appointment in your calendars. You don't want to leave it up to chance with a note on the back of a business card; it might not make it into their calendar. Ask "if I send you an email confirming our appointment, will you be able to get back to me or would it be better if I call you?" These days many people prefer email as they can get to it when they have a moment; it's right there next to their calendar, and it's easy to reply back to you.

When you do go out with them, don't use that time to give a sales pitch; use this as a time to get to know about them and find out about their hobbies and strengthen that relationship. This is also a great way for you to get ideas for who you can introduce them to in your network. This increases your likeability factor and the value you are adding to the relationship.

9. Take your offline networking online

Ask people if they are on Facebook or Twitter and if they'd like to connect with you online. Then, over the course of the month connect with them through your social networks. Comment on their page and let them know that you enjoyed speaking with them at the Chamber of Commerce event.

If you see them posting comments about something to do with their hobby or a great book that they've read, that would be another great area to comment on. Then, when you see them at the next in-person event, your relationship with them will have grown and you'll have more to talk about. By taking your offline networking strategy online, by connecting with people from in-person networking events on the social networks, you will deepen those relationships.

10. Follow-up, follow-up, follow-up!

Follow-up is key! For the people you made a connection with, take the time to follow up with a personally written greeting card. You don't want to pick up all the cards from the brochure table and start sending out marketing material. Rather, take the cards of the several people you had conversations with that day and follow up with a greeting card to let them know how much you enjoyed meeting them and that you look forward to seeing them again soon. If you feel inspired and believe it is a good use of your time, you may want to invite them to get together for coffee or lunch.

Sending greeting cards to people you meet is a fantastic way to build relationships. They will keep your cards and they'll think of you. The art of the handwritten greeting card, up until recently, has pretty much been lost. More and more we hear about the importance of handwritten cards and there seems to be a revival of this practice. There are stories of incredibly successful sales people who built their business by keeping in touch through heartfelt cards.

Online networking and in-person networking are key to your relationship marketing strategy and building strong business relationships.

Action Steps

Here are seven steps that you can take to put what you've learned into action.

1. Set up your professional profile on Facebook, LinkedIn, and Twitter. Develop a branded profile across the social networks.
2. Link your Facebook and LinkedIn accounts to Twitter. Each time you tweet, your message will also show up on Facebook and LinkedIn.
3. On LinkedIn, join at least two interest groups and start your own group.
4. On Facebook, set up a fan page representing your business, service, product, or program.
5. On Twitter, customize your profile with your branded colors and schedule time to tweet at least once a week.
6. Attend a local networking group in your town and apply some of the in-person networking tips that you learned in this chapter.
7. Connect on Facebook with at least three of your in-person networking contacts.

Resources Mentioned in This Chapter

Facebook: www.Facebook.com
Twitter: www.Twitter.com
LinkedIn: www.LinkedIn.com
Blitz Time: www.BlitzTime.com
Social Marketing: www.SocialNetworksToday.com
Hoot Suite: www.HootSuite.com

Keep in Touch, Keep in Mind

Keeping in touch with people in a variety of ways will make them feel special and appreciated. This practice is one of the most powerful things you can do to build business relationships. In addition to using the phone, there are many ways that you can keep in touch, by harnessing the power of the written word, while building trust and credibility.

Easy Ways to Keep in Touch

If people know that the content they'll be receiving from you can help them to grow their businesses, they will make it a priority to read what you send them. Here are several practical examples of ways to harness the power of the written word:

69

- Send personalized, brief, follow-up email to people you meet.
- Set up an auto responder system to keep your clients and prospects close.
- Send out a weekly or a monthly ezine, packed with value and helpful ideas.
- Deliver your course material via your own eCourse.
- Send handwritten greeting cards on a regular basis.

Send Personalized Email

Email is an essential tool and, when used properly, can be a great way to share information and keep in touch. However, email has gotten out of control, and the majority of business owners who communicate through email are overwhelmed with the vast amount they receive each day. Thus, you also want to find other, more impactful, ways to communicate with your audience.

While it is a handy way to keep in touch with people you know, or to ask a quick question of a friend or colleague, email is no longer effective as a marketing tool or as a way of building relationships. You cannot send an email to a large group of people from your own email account without a high risk of being flagged as a spammer and thus causing your messages to be banned.

When composing your email messages, keep them brief, leave white space between paragraphs, make sure your subject lines are specific and personalized and keep the number of questions you ask to a minimum. These practices will increase the likelihood of a reply.

Auto Responder

An auto responder is a reliable way to get email delivered to a large group of people on a regular basis. You set up a welcome email to start and then you can decide how often you'd like your messages to go out. Auto responders are a great way to educate customers and clients, support your team, nurture people on your list, and build trust with your prospects.

In order for someone to receive your auto responder messages, they need to subscribe to your list. By doing so, they are giving you permission to communicate with them. The services that are most widely used and recommended by Internet marketers are AWeber (www.WebmailConnections.com) and 1ShoppingCart (www.BestShoppingCartSystem.com). With these services, you can either program the system so that when people opt-in they are automatically added to your list, or you can select the double opt-in method. With the double opt-in method, when someone signs up to receive your auto responder messages, they will receive an email asking that they click a link to confirm their request to be added to your list. This is called a double opt-in and ensures that either you or someone else did not subscribe the reader without their permission. By requiring that your subscribers double opt-in, you also protect yourself from false spam reports.

As you develop your own list you'll find that the more quality content you offer, the more people will remain on your list. If someone decides to unsubscribe, there is no reason to take it personally. It could be that they simply are receiving too much email and need to streamline. With this in mind and in regards to the email that you receive, you may want to open up a free Gmail account (www.Gmail.com) that you designate specifically for Web subscriptions. This way you can go in and read the messages after work hours and be able to better enjoy the content.

Ezine

An ezine is an online magazine or newsletter. It can be sent out weekly or monthly. It can be in plain text and easy to read even on a cell phone, or it can be pretty and colorful, with images and in your branded colors. Your ezine should not be a "sales pitch" but rather a friendly correspondence between you and your readers. Let them know what exciting ventures are going on in your life, share a cute or funny story, and deliver quality educational content. Then you can let them know what courses you have coming up or what products you are currently promoting. Build relationships and create raving fans!

ECourse

An eCourse is a course that you deliver via email. You set it up in AWeber, or in whichever system you choose to use, and decide how often you'd like the content to go out. An eCourse is course content and not sales letters or calendar notifications. You can include information that is part of your eCourse, but you want to maintain the integrity of your list and focus on giving subscribers the content they are expecting. Let them know that their course will be delivered via email once a week for the duration of the course. A very effective way to deliver your content is by posting it in a member's area and providing the link to the new module or the course content area, via a weekly auto responder message. Thus, eCourse content can be delivered exclusively via email or it can serve as a notification for your members to head over to the member's area to access the next module.

Direct Mail

Direct mail is another powerful way to keep in touch and stay in the minds of the people who matter most to you. If you plan on marketing online, then you have the opportunity to set yourself apart from the average person by sending a card to your students or customers to let them know you appreciate them. When was the last time you received a thank-you card or an instructional card after purchasing a product or a course? Scheduling time each day to send out a heartfelt card of appreciation will make a huge difference in your life and in your business.

The Power of the Handwritten Greeting Card

The art of writing good old-fashioned greeting cards is alive and well in today's business environment.

There is nothing like a handwritten card. If you read the stories of some of the most successful business people of all times, they will share with you that sending personally written greeting cards has played a large part in their success.

Tom Hopkins, an international sales trainer, sent ten cards a day when he was in the real estate industry. He shares that after three years of doing this, 100 percent of his business came from referrals. Tom promotes the habit of sending ten cards a day. Of his suggested reasons for sending a card, my favorite is, "send a card to the person who did **not** purchase from you." By keeping in touch with these people, the next time they have a need for your service they will likely think of you and want to do business with you because you are the one that kept in touch with them.

Joe Girard, who is listed in the *Guinness Book of World Records* as the "World's Greatest Salesman" for 12 years running, attributes his success to having sent twelve cards a year to each person on his customer list. His customers looked forward to receiving his cards each month and when it came time for them to purchase a new automobile, whom do you think they thought of?

If you practice relationship marketing and let your prospects and clients know that you care about them, they will look forward to hearing from you. If these two men can be at the top of their game by using handwritten greeting cards, just think of what keeping in closer contact with your prospects and clients can do for your business!

Send Greeting Cards, Not Marketing Pieces in Business Envelopes

Think about how you feel when you get a card from someone, especially when it's a heartfelt card. When you get your mail, what is the first thing you do? It is not uncommon for mail to be opened near a garbage can. The first thing people do is discard the junk, set the bills aside, and look for the "good stuff."

You want to be part of the "good stuff." You want people to smile and laugh and feel good when they read you card. There's no better way to do it than to get an actual greeting card in their hands. Whether you use a card from the supermarket or your stationery drawer or you use a service like SendOutCards (www.CardsYouRemember.com) where you can create your cards online and they mail them out for you, creating the habit of writing greeting cards each day will have a powerful and positive impact on your business.

The service that I use is SendOutCards. They have thousands of cards to choose from and offer the ability to add your own photos as well as your handwriting font and signature. You are also able to send a gift with your card. From gourmet gift baskets to motivational books, they have a wide range of options to choose from. You create your card online and once you click the send button, they stamp and mail your card for you.

This system was designed to be a tool that people could use to act on their promptings. When you have a prompting to reach out to someone, you can quickly and easily send that person a heartfelt card. So many times we think of someone and maybe that person's name goes onto a sticky note. We have the best intentions to reach out and call or send a card, but, unfortunately, many of those names on sticky notes end up getting thrown away.

I've always written thank you notes, though sometimes I would fall behind. I had the best of intentions and sometimes I would even get as far as filling out the envelope. Inevitably many of these cards would get buried on my desk. I'm so grateful to have found a system that can automate this process for me. Take note that it is never too late to send a thank-you or appreciation card. Even if you need to apologize for your card arriving late, it will uplift the recipient and strengthen your relationships.

I've often heard people say that they can't afford to send out greeting cards and that they send email because it doesn't cost them anything. My question to you is, "what price tag can you put on the value of a prospect or a client?" Consider taking the "Greeting Card Challenge." Select a segment of your list. Send them a thank-you card for purchasing your product or enrolling in your course. If you spent about $100 on greeting cards to reach 100 people, how many sales would you need to make to break even? Make your cards informative and fun and invite the recipients to take a specific action. The more you make people smile, the more they will pay attention to what you are saying. Take this challenge and track your numbers: Prepare to be amazed!

Getting your heartfelt card into someone's hands is a powerful way to reach out and connect with him/her. That person will remember you and keep these cards! Make sure that if you are sending a heartfelt card that the card is all about them and your appreciation for them. You will lose the effectiveness if you try to sell them or ask them for something (like referrals) in this card. You certainly also want to send out marketing pieces, but they should not be mixed in with your heartfelt cards of appreciation.

If you send birthday cards, you'll notice that people will thank you in person or by sending you a card thanking you for the birthday card. You'll also find that some people will pick up the phone to let you know how much they appreciate your card. In the words of Kody Bateman, founder and CEO of SendOutCards, "Make a living through giving!"

Send Greeting Cards to Your Online Customers

For those who sell a product or service via the Internet, taking your relationship offline and giving someone something tangible that they can hold in their hands builds loyalty and a strong bond between you and your customers. People keep cards, especially if they make them smile.

You can even send a packet of flower seeds to your business contacts and associates and say something like, "planting the seeds of success." Again, when you bring a smile to someone's face, you bring a smile to his or her heart, and you become memorable and appreciated.

Sending heartfelt greeting cards has helped me build relationships and increase my sales. I use greeting cards as a tool for thanking my customers and notifying them of new products. I also use cards as a way for delivering training tips to my team.

With handwritten letters and cards becoming extinct, most people will be delighted to receive a real greeting card. Email can often get ignored, deleted, or lost, but people keep greeting cards, especially if there is a picture of something personal to them on the card.

15 Occasions for Sending Greeting Cards

1. Holidays, birthdays, and special occasions
2. Customer appreciation
3. Nice to meet you
4. Thank you for product purchases
5. Anniversary of their purchase or membership
6. Product knowledge
7. Product reorder reminder
8. Special sales and promotions
9. New course offerings
10. Thank you for the referral
11. Recognition
12. Training
13. Congratulations on their presentation, promotion or accomplishments
14. Introduction to someone you are referring
15. Welcome to the team

Action Steps

Here are seven steps that you can take to put what you've learned into action.

1. Open up a Gmail email account (www.Gmail.com) for online subscriptions.
2. Open up an account at AWeber (www.WebmailConnections.com) or at 1ShoppingCart (www.BestShoppingCartSystem.com), if you don't yet have an auto responder service.
3. Set up your first auto responder list and post the list opt-in form on your blog sidebar.
4. Use your auto responder service and create a customer, team, or members ezine.
5. Develop an eCourse on a topic that you feel your subscribers would enjoy; each module can be as short as a few paragraphs in length and be programmed to be delivered weekly via your auto responder service.
6. Make a list of your top fifty customers and/or prospects and put their birthdays in your calendar. Make it a habit to send each of them a birthday card, each year.
7. Make it a habit to mail at least one personally written greeting card each day.

Resources Mentioned in This Chapter

AWeber: www.WebmailConnections.com
Gmail: www.Gmail.com
SendOutCards: www.CardsYouRemember.com
1ShoppingCart: www.BestShoppingCartSystem.com

Turn Your Message into Money with Teleseminars

You connect with your audience with your voice. One way to build relationships is for people to hear your voice because they can hear your enthusiasm. They get a sense of who you are. They feel your energy and they get to know you. Offering teleseminars is an extremely effective way to accomplish this. Additionally, as you will see in the next chapter, your teleseminar transcript serves as the foundation for being able to create numerous products from the same content.

What Is a Teleseminar?

A teleseminar is a **seminar** conducted over a **telephone**, set up as a conference call. On your teleseminar, you can either speak via a muted line, thus cutting out all background noise, or you can set up your call to allow audience participation. You can even set up your call to allow one or more guest speakers. For those not able to attend the live call you can create an MP3 recording of your teleseminar. Thus, people have the option of listening online or downloading the recording to their computer.

Teleseminars can be a one-time event or a series of calls. They can be free or you can charge for them. You can allow free attendance to the live event and charge for the replay. There are any number of options here. One popular model is where you offer a teleseminar series with four or five modules, delivered once or twice a week. You can provide an action guide or study guide for the attendees so that they retain the information better and are more attentive. These can be very profitable on their own and are invaluable as a source of content that you can repurpose into a wide variety of additional information products. Teleseminars are a fantastic way for you to share your expertise with a large group of people at one time.

Teleseminars provide you with a powerful way to:

1. Share your message and develop a following,
2. Create material that can be repurposed,

3. Offer an online seminar series on your topic or book,
4. Hold a weekly class or Q & A session, and
5. Educate your clients or your team

Following, you'll find several options for the recording and delivery of your teleseminars.

Free Conference Calling

My favorite free option is Free Conference Calling (www.FreeConferenceCalling.com). The reason I recommend this service is because they have a Web application that allows you to see the names and phone numbers of your attendees. Your attendees also have the ability to punch in a code to indicate that they have a question or are responding to a question you are asking. Your call recordings are hosted on the Free Conference Calling site and you can even post a link to allow your audience to access either single recordings or all of the recordings in a series. They give you the ability to download the recording to your computer. I recommend that you download each call and you put it someplace safe. While your account is open, you can link straight to your call archives area. But if you ever cancel your account, all of your recordings will be on that system, and they would be lost. So download copies of the recordings just to be safe.

Blog Talk Radio

Another way to get your message out across the Internet is to set up an online radio show on

BlogTalkRadio (www.BlogTalkRadio.com). This is a free platform that gets a lot of traffic. This is also a fun way to build your name brand recognition and become known as an expert in your field. Once you've recorded your first show, you can download a widget to place on your blog or Web site. This will make your content readily available to your community.

When you set up your account, be sure to strategically pick your user name, as that is going to be your station name and what people type in as part of the Web address. Select something that reflects your business or the topic that you'll be speaking on. BlogTalkRadio has an option that allows you to easily and automatically send the replay of your broadcast over to iTunes.

While BlogTalkRadio is a fantastic platform, it may not be best for every situation. If you broadcast on BlogTalkRadio, your content is free and available to anyone and everyone. If you want to maintain the proprietary rights to that you want to sell, then you're not going to want to publish the whole program on BlogTalkRadio. You can use BlogTalkRadio to leverage a preview show. In this way you get the benefit of lots of exposure and the ability to invite people to your site to learn more about you and your programs. I would only use this method on occasion, though, as you'll want to give substantial content to your listeners so that they come back and tell others about your show.

Webcast Platform with InstantTeleseminar

The most popular premium teleseminar service is
the InstantTeleseminar platform
(www.WebTeleSeminars.com). In addition to being
able to record and rebroadcast your recording, you
can see the call-in details of each of your attendees,
conduct polls, offer a Webcast option to your
listeners, show PowerPoint presentations, and have
an instant Web site where people can go to listen in
live or to listen or view the replay afterwards. The
Webcast option is great if your listeners are across
the globe and for those who don't want to tie up their
phone line. It also provides the ability to reach a
much larger audience because you are not limited by
the number of callers on the phone lines. They offer
a free trial to test out the service and hold a few
teleseminars in order to experience all they have to
offer first-hand. You can cancel your trial or your
subscription at any point just by sending an email to
their support system. They have excellent customer
support.

You can use the service to reach listeners anywhere
in the world. They can call into your teleseminar
number or they can listen to the Webcast via the
Internet. The Webcast option is quite popular
because it offers the listener more flexibility.

The downside of the Webcast option is when the
speaker opens up the call and asks for questions,
those on the Webcast will not be heard. However,
they do have the ability to submit their questions via
a text box on the Webcast page. This service can

expand your audience because you can have an unlimited number who can access the Webcast.

Each call session has its own Web page, which you can customize from a wide selection of colorful options. The Webcast page actually looks like a custom-designed Web page. Your listeners go there to get the call details, such as the time, date, and phone number, as well as access to the Webcast page. The ability to add Web links and a big button to your Webcast page is another great feature. You can offer people the action guide for your teleseminar or a free downloadable report as well as access to your blog, social networks, or your Web site, etc.

Your First Teleseminar

For your first teleseminar, you may want to simply invite some friends or family members to attend. Deliver your message while live people are on the call with you. There's something very powerful about delivering your message to a live audience that you can't capture when you're recording at home by yourself. When you have attendees with you on the call, you can't say, "wait a minute let me rewind that." This causes you to keep moving forward and sharing your message. You can always edit the audio recording and the transcripts afterwards. Once you've done this a few times, you'll be a pro. You get more comfortable as time goes on.

Remember we're a busy society and people have busy schedules. The flexibility of the teleseminar format allows listeners to listen to the call live or afterwards via the recording. If people are not able to attend your live call, you should never take it personally. People have busy schedules. Make the content as accessible as possible for as many people as possible in as many ways as possible.

Make it easy for your audience to access your material. Let them know ahead of time that while it is preferable for them to be on the call live, that if for whatever reason, they aren't able to make the live teleseminar, they'll be able to access the recording afterward. Another great way to share your message is by podcasting your teleseminars on iTunes. This is very easy to do and you can choose whether to offer your content for free or whether you want to charge people to download it from iTunes.

By making the recording accessible to your audience after the call, you make it easy for them to consume and absorb the content. For those who were not able to attend live, they can listen to the recording afterward. Some people will listen online while others will download the recording to their iPod or burn a CD to listen to in the car. The more ways you can get your content into the hands of your audience the better off you are. This gives your audience greater access to your knowledge and products and gives you the opportunity for building stronger relationships with them.

Monetize Your Teleseminars

That brings us to what you can do to monetize your teleseminars, thus earning income from selling related products. Let's explore what you can do with this material to bring value to your audience and brand yourself as an expert in your field. The term "repurposing" is a term that is becoming known in Internet marketing circles. An example of repurposing would be, as in the above example, providing an MP3 recording of your call. Another example would be for you to provide the transcript of your call. How powerful would it be for someone in your target audience to not only have listened in on your call, but to receive a printable transcript that they can review at their convenience?

Taking this a step further, what if you were to take your transcripts and break them into smaller chunks, which can either become the foundation for an eBook or manual or can be used as part of your weekly email training? There are many ways that you can repurpose material in order to brand yourself and offer more value to your audience.

One way to easily monetize your teleseminar is to offer an "upsell" once someone registers to attend. In addition to being able to listen to the recorded call online, offer them the ability to purchase the MP3 download and the transcript.

Consider your costs as you are determining what you will charge. For example, it will cost you between $60 and $130 to have an hour-long recording transcribed by a professional service. Your MP3 recording is free. Figure out how many attendees you will need in order to cover your costs. Anything above that is profit.

In the next chapter we will be going into great detail as to what you can do with your teleseminar recordings. Here are just a few things that you can do with the recordings and transcripts from your teleseminars:

- Use the replay itself as a blog post.
- Create a free report.
- Use the content as part of an eCourse series.
- Turn the transcript into articles.
- Create PowerPoint presentations and create video articles.

Ways to Promote Your Teleseminar

Spread the word to your email list and your contacts on the social networks that you are holding a teleseminar or teleseminar series. Offer this for free and let people know that everyone is invited to attend; all they need to do is register. Let them know that, if they register, even if they cannot make the live event, they will receive the replay link.

Set up a list in your AWeber or auto responder system. Post the opt-in form on a page of your blog and encourage people to register for information and call in details for your teleseminar. Their information will go into your auto responder system, which will allow you to send out a message thanking them for registering. You can also send out the call details and reminders the week before, the day before and the day of your teleseminar.

After the teleseminar, you can send out the replay link. If you have provided the live teleseminar for free, provide a way for people to listen to the replay online. On the replay page you can have a gentle invitation inviting people to purchase the MP3 recording and transcripts if they'd like to be able to access the material offline.

Now that these subscribers are on your list, you can drip valuable content to them as well as invitations to future teleseminars. These contacts are going to stay on your list because they want to access your content and connect with you and your community. The greatest asset of your online business is your list. If you nurture and feed your list, they are going to want to hear from you and they are going to want to learn from you.

Tips and Hints

When you are speaking to a large group of people, as a rule you want to mute the call. Otherwise you are going to have pots and pans clanging, dogs barking, people talking, and a lot of other noise in the background, which can be very frustrating for you and your listeners. Also be sure to disable your call waiting so that no beeps are heard or recorded.

Teleseminar Interviews

Interviews provide incredible content for a teleseminar series in your topic area. You could then sell those interviews individually or as part of a series. You can allow people to listen from your Web site or to be able to download the audio and transcripts. You can have your own interview series on your interest topic and that could become valuable content for your members.

Ideas for Teleseminar Topics

- Q & A teleseminar where your audience either asks you live questions or you answer questions that have been submitted in writing
- Expert interview teleseminar where you feature speakers on topics related to your topic and/or topics that your audience is interested in
- Book review teleseminars
- Product review teleseminars
- Educational course delivered via teleseminar
- Team training teleseminar
- Sales presentation teleseminar
- Product knowledge and training teleseminar
- Fishbowl hot-seat teleseminar where you give personalized attention to an individual while others get to listen in and benefit
- Group mastermind or brainstorming session teleseminar

Teleseminars are very effective in getting your message out to solve the challenges that your audience is facing and for you to become that known expert in your field.

Take the step to hold your first teleseminar. Take notes as to what went well and what you'd do differently. Continue to hold teleseminars, perhaps on a weekly or monthly basis, as practicing will ensure you get better and better. Just like anything in life, you'll get better with practice.

Action Steps

Here are seven steps that you can take to put what you've learned into action.

1. Decide which service you will use for your teleseminars.
2. Write down a list of ideas that you would like to speak on.
3. Select a topic for your first teleseminar.
4. Set up and prepare for your teleseminar.
5. Promote your teleseminar and build your list by having people opt-in to receive access to the call recording page.
6. Hold your teleseminar; be sure to record it.
7. Send an auto responder message out to those who registered letting them know how they can listen to the call recording online.

Resources Mentioned in This Chapter

Free Conference Calling:
www.FreeConferenceCalling.com
BlogTalkRadio: www.BlogTalkRadio.com
InstantTeleseminar: www.WebTeleSeminars.com

Repurposing Your Content for Multiple Paydays

We each have a limited number of hours in a day. If you are in a profession where you get paid by the hour, your income is limited by the number of hours you can work. If, however, you leverage your time and develop ways to create passive income, you get paid over and over again for work you did yesterday or on the work that others are doing on your behalf. An example of this is when you get paid a commission on the work that your staff completes.

Active Income and Passive Income

A way to maximize your passive income is to build a team in a network marketing company. This is an excellent way to build passive income as you get paid over and over again, not only on the work that you do, but also on the work that your team is doing.

You can generate a passive income on the Internet when you create a product and turn it into multiple products, thus getting paid several times on the same content. This process is called repurposing. Some people prefer to read while others like to listen to a CD in their car and still others would prefer to view a video. Why not provide all of these options and give people a variety of products to choose from?

If you are a specialist, such as a professional organizer, coach, therapist, or photographer and you are billing for the services you are providing, you only have so many hours in a day. It does not matter whether you are a heart surgeon or a high-priced attorney, you are still only able to bill for the time you are working. What if the attorney, heart surgeon, professional organizer, or business coach could take their knowledge and turn that into content that people could ingest in a wide variety of ways. They could then be paid over and over again for this content.

Recorded Interviews

A fantastic source of content is an audio-recorded interview. You can interview people who are experts in your topic area or whose message your audience would love to hear. Transcribe the audio recordings and use them in a variety of ways. Here are some suggestions for how to do this:

- Offer the transcripts to your subscribers.
- Sell the transcripts to people who attend your interview series.
- Create a simple PowerPoint presentation to accompany the audio and turn it into a screen capture video.
- Create a collection of related interviews and sell the audios and transcripts individually or as a collection.
- Offer the transcripts alongside the companion video as another product.
- Chunk your transcripts into smaller segments and you'll have content for articles, blog posts, or even for an eCourse.

Find a way to take what you know and what you can teach people and put it into different formats so that it is available for sale, 24/7, on your Web site. You may be off on vacation and yet people can come to your site where you have packaged your expertise in a variety of ways, at several price points, and they can buy your content through an automated process that you set up. This is a fabulous example of passive income: You are not working directly with a client, yet you are still making money.

Online Interviews as a Source of Rich and Vibrant Content

One of the easiest and most effective ways to generate relevant and pertinent content is to do an audio interview series. By doing so you will be providing valuable content to your audience while building relationships with the people you interview. I have developed a deeper relationship with each person that I have interviewed on my online radio show and my listeners are really enjoying the content.

Some of the questions that people ask about developing an audio interview series are:

- Who do I interview?
- How do I record the interview?
- What questions do I ask of the person being interviewed?
- What do I do with the audio recordings?

Who to Interview

The interests of your audience should define who you interview and what you discuss with them. For example, my audience is made up of business professionals and entrepreneurs who want to learn more about blogging and marketing their businesses online. When looking for people to interview, I look for people who are experts in these areas. This provides my guest speakers with exposure to a new audience while giving my listeners relevant and pertinent content.

It could be that you already know people who speak on topics of interest to your audience. If not, you can visit LinkedIn and Facebook groups on your niche topic and take note of who is posting articles and answering questions in a way that adds value to that community. Another place to locate relevant content and connect with potential speakers is at Ezine Articles (www.EzineArticles.com). Do a search on potential topics and then spend some time reviewing the articles and visiting the Web sites of the authors.

How to Record the Interview

As mentioned in the previous chapter, there are many options available for recording your interviews. Whichever service you use, spend some time reading through their documentation and set up a test interview with a friend or business associate. Create a podcast of your calls or your call series and download the MP3 of your interview.

What Questions to Ask During the Interview

To date, I have conducted more than 40 interviews. Fortunately, before I began my online radio show I was a guest on someone else's show. Before the interview I was asked to provide a typed list of eight to ten prioritized questions. This has proved to be an invaluable tool for me. By asking each of my guests to provide a list of their prioritized questions, based on a topic that we agree upon ahead of time, they are prepared and are able to speak about things that they are knowledgeable of and passionate about.

What to do with Your Interviews

So what do you do with these interviews? It depends on if you're selling them all at once or individually or if you are giving them away. Some people use a series as a bonus giveaway for people joining their program. You can offer your interview recordings as an incentive for people subscribing to your list. Invite people to enter their name and email address in order to receive a weekly interview with an expert, or you can simply use these interviews as content for your blog.

The first thing you want to do is have your interviews transcribed. I highly recommend that you have them transcribed by a professional service that only employs native English speaking transcriptionists. When I first got started online I would outsource my audios to be transcribed by a service overseas. As nice as the people were, English was not their native language and it would take me hours to clean up each transcript.

Transcription services offer a wide variety of options. The options can consist of a straightforward transcript or transcription that is already formatted as an eBook. They can also break the transcript up further so it becomes content for your eCourse, articles, or blog posts. You can also take a blog post and use the content for creating a couple of slides in PowerPoint. You can create a video recording of that PowerPoint presentation using Jing Project or Camtasia Studio, and turn it into a video. Now you have a video article that can be uploaded to YouTube or to your blog.

From eBooks to videos, there are a wide variety of products that can easily be produced from your repurposed teleseminar transcript. Not to worry! You do not need to be a "techie" in order to apply these suggestions. Have fun, be creative, and think outside of the box. There are people who will greatly benefit by hearing your message, even if it seems second nature to you. They will gladly pay you to share it with them. Offering a wide range of options not only provides additional revenue sources for you, it also makes your message more accessible and easy for more people to digest. Here is a spectrum of ideas for you to choose from.

1. eBooks
2. MP3 recordings
3. CD recordings
4. eCourses
5. Workbooks
6. Blog posts
7. Articles
8. Newsletters
9. Home study courses
10. PowerPoint Video presentations

eBook

You can easily turn you transcript into an eBook. Simply add a footer with your name and Web site, add a title page, table of contents, author page, and a resource page and you are good to go. A disclaimer page can also be added in the beginning part of your eBook. This page will specify whether or not it is legal to make copies or distribute your eBook. Also added on this page are your copyright and your company information. You can also provide a Web site or email address to encourage individuals to inform you if they have received your book from another place other than your site. It is simply used as to discourage illegal copying and is wise to include in your eBook.

The ideal recommended length for an eBook is about seventy-five pages, though you can easily create an eBook from twenty-five to one hundred and seventy-five pages in length. Any less than twenty-five pages and you may want to call your work a "report" and any longer than seventy-five pages discourages people from printing out your eBook.

Ways to Monetize Your eBook and Audio Recordings

Your eBook can be included as part of course content and included with registration for your teleseminar. You can also charge for your eBook as an upsell for those who register for your teleseminars.

Your eBook can also be made available through your Web site. Simply have a graphic designer develop an eBook image of your book and arrange to have that shown on your Web site with a link to a shopping cart to purchase the item. You can take it a step further and offer it with an affiliate incentive. Other people will promote and sell your eBook for an affiliate percentage. Your eBook will get more exposure and you will make money as well as help others make some extra income.

MP3 Recordings

Your audio recordings are an excellent way to market your brand, service, and/or product. You can host your recordings on your Web site or blog and stream them through iTunes. You can either use a WordPress plugin such as Podpress to add a podcast to your WordPress blog or use the services of BlogTalkRadio.

CD Recordings

Once you have your digital eBook, you can then turn it into a CD. The CD can have you simply reading the content, or you may want to add musical accompaniment at the beginning and end of chapters for a more professional feel. There are several options available to create a CD from your eBook or transcripts. There is a service called Kunaki (www.Kunaki.com), which allows you to upload your audio or video recording along with digital images for the cover and the top of the disc. They will transform the information into CD or DVD format. You can set up an order form so that people can purchase your DVDs or your CDs. Kunaki currently charges $1.75 per disc and case and they'll deliver to the customer for you. You don't have to spend thousands of dollars and have a warehouse full of CDs in your garage or in your basement.

eCourse

You can create an eCourse, and deliver it via email over a specific period of time. As mentioned previously, the services most highly recommended by Internet marketers for email delivery are 1ShoppingCart (www.BestShoppingCartSystem.com) and AWeber (www.WebmailConnections.com). With these services you can program how often you want your email, eCourse, or ezine to go out. This is called an auto responder. For the purposes of your eCourse, you may want the content to be delivered every day or once a week for a specific period of time.

Both AWeber and 1ShoppingCart are simple to use and they have a library of training videos as well as exceptional customer service. Once you set up your account, you can set up as many lists as you like. You can have lists for different products or courses as well as a different list for each of your blogs or Web sites. Once you've set up your list, you'll want to create a message inviting people to click the link to acknowledge that they've requested information from you. They call this a double opt-in method and what this does is protect you from potential spam complaints, which could jeopardize your online presence. You may want to set up the double opt-in option because it will protect you. If someone makes a spam complaint, AWeber or 1ShoppingCart can come back and say, "I'm sorry but we have proof that you double opted in and you can easily just unsubscribe."

Once someone opts in to your list, they will automatically receive the first message in the series. Be sure to set up your messages and program them to go out at the desired frequency. Again, there are very helpful tutorials available to you that will get you up to speed.

What I like to do with the first message in the series is welcome the subscriber, let them know what they can look forward to, and invite them to visit the site. This first message is what goes out immediately after they confirm their subscription.

Once you have your subscription opt-in and your first message set up, you can create a custom opt-in form for your site. There are a wide variety of designs to choose from so that your opt-in form has the look and feel of your branded image. Once you create the form, you copy the code and you pop it into a widget on the sidebar of your blog. Web opt-in forms are highly customizable and easy to set up and maintain.

Workbooks and Action Guides

Use content from your course to create questions for people to think through and think about. Workbooks (which can also be called Action Guides) include key points, essential information, and fill-in-the-blank lines. They also provide space for people to take notes on what they are learning. It is very simple to add a workbook to anything you are doing. It adds value to your course. A workbook also helps people consume your information because they are not just listening to or reading what you have, but they are answering questions for themselves. Workbooks are a very simple product to create.

103

Blog Posts

Blog posts can provide information about your interests, products, or services. Your blog is your platform from where you can share your message and your passions. Make it a habit to write several times a week, even if just for thirty minutes at a time. To make the posts more interesting, remember to add photos and break up the paragraphs with bullet points or different headings.

Articles

Your blog posts can be turned into articles by adding more content. The articles can then be distributed on different article directories such as Ezine Articles. Marketing with articles is simple and very cost effective. You can either write the articles yourself, pulling from transcripts or audios you have developed, or you can outsource to a ghostwriter to write for you.

Ezine Articles

To create more credibility and become known as an expert in your field, you'll want to set up an account at Ezine Articles (www.EzineArticles.com) and begin publishing articles on a regular basis. When you set up your account you will be able to set up your bio and your signature box. This is your opportunity to share about you and invite people to your site. Your signature line will show up automatically at the end of each of your articles. Be sure to review the guidelines and tutorials, as they are very helpful and informative.

Ezine Articles is a place where people can share their wisdom, expertise, findings, reviews of products, and reviews of books with one another. This is, in essence, an article repository. If someone is looking for an article on a specific topic for their blog or ezine, they can use the published articles on the site. There are guidelines for using this content such as keeping any links "live" so that when your viewers click on them they go to where the author intends for them to go. Again, you can read the specifics at Ezine Articles.

Once your account is set up, you will receive your own author page on the site. This is where all of your articles will be listed. You can also use an Ezine Articles widget on your Web site so that your visitors can see your article feed and easily access any of your published articles. You may want to set up a URL — such as "www.ArticlesByDvorah.com"— so that you can easily direct your audience to your page on Ezine Articles. An easy way to create articles is to use portions of your transcribed teleseminars.

Article Bio Box: Tips for Getting People to Your Web Site

When you are wrapping up your article, you don't want to say "in conclusion" because what you're saying is "Okay, goodbye. You can leave now; you don't need to go to my Web site. We're done." You want your articles to lead into your bio box in a way that seems like it is a continuation of your article and worded in a way that encourages people to go to your site. One example is to say, "For additional articles (or a special report) on this topic visit our blog at..." In your bio box, do not tell them all about you and how wonderful you are, but do include your name and credentials along with an invitation to your Web site.

Integrating Your Ezine Articles Site with Your Social Networks

You can set up your Ezine Articles site so it automatically notifies Twitter that you have just published a new article. By linking up your Twitter account with Facebook and LinkedIn, all three social networks will be notified each time you publish a new article.

Newsletters

If you have written content from newsletters that you've published over the years, you can easily repurpose those articles. You can also draw from your teleseminar course and interviews as another great source of content for your newsletter.

Home Study Courses

Information that you have created in audio, video, or written form can all be re-purposed into a home study course. The information can be transcribed and developed into an eBook form or simply an eCourse that can be delivered digitally via email.

PowerPoint Video Presentations

You can create a PowerPoint presentation, and use screen capture software such as Camtasia (www.techsmith.com/camtasia.asp) or Jing Project (www.JingProject.com) to make it a video. You could even use your Webcam to make a smaller box inside your PowerPoint with you talking about the presentation. They call this feature a "picture-in-picture". We will discuss these formats in more depth in Chapter Seven.

You are not limited by geography anymore. The whole world can consume what you have to teach because you have put it out there on the Internet. Have fun, be creative and enjoy creating several streams of income from the same content.

Action Steps

Here are seven steps that you can take to put what you've learned into action.

1. Have one of your teleseminars transcribed.
2. Turn the transcript into an eBook.
3. Take a copy of your eBook and extract five to ten articles for a digitally delivered eCourse, using your auto responder service.
4. Take a copy of your eBook and divide it up into articles and blog posts.
5. Go through your articles and select some of them for your upcoming newsletter.
6. Create a PowerPoint presentation from one of your articles and make a video recording using the free software at Jing Project (www.JingProject.com).
7. Upload your MP3 recording to Kunaki (www.Kunaki.com) and create a CD.

Resources Mentioned in This Chapter

Articles by D'vorah: www.ArticlesByDvorah.com

Ezine Articles: www.EzineArticles.com

Jing Project: www.JingProject.com

Kunaki: www.Kunaki.com

AWeber: www.WebmailConnections.com

Camtasia: www.techsmith.com/camtasia.asp

Video Is a Powerful
Relationship Building Tool

Video is the most effective way to connect with your audience, as they can both see and hear you. Video allows them to get to know you and is an amazing tool for building trust and building relationships.

Web video is the hottest thing on the Internet right now and it will be for many years to come. It's more powerful than audio and easier now than ever before to create.

There are several options for creating Web video. You can have a Webcam on your computer and create a "talking head" type of video where your viewers see you on the screen. You can also create video with a Flip camera or a camcorder; most new digital photo cameras will also record video. This allows you to capture live footage of anything you'd like to share with your viewers.

Another type of video is called screen capture video. You can easily create video tutorials with screen capture video. You can select a portion of your computer screen to be shown and verbally share your message with your viewing audience.

Video Marketing

Video is an excellent way to market on the Internet and a fantastic way to keep viewers on your site longer. There is a debate as to whether or not to have your video auto-start when someone arrives at your site. It depends on the site and what your purpose is in having people visit.

For sales pages where you are encouraging people to either purchase something or opt-in to your mailing list, having a video that automatically starts when someone gets to your sales page is recommended. You will capture their attention and they are more likely to explore further.

If, on the other hand, you are driving people to an information site that you want them to visit frequently, then it is perhaps better that your videos do not automatically begin. When people want to view your videos, they can click the easily accessible start arrow.

The most common complaint with regard to audios or videos starting automatically is that they can startle the listener who may click to get away from your site. View your site from the eyes of your visitors and give thought as to how you would feel, based on what you see and hear.

Almost any type of product or service can be promoted through video, but it's important to do it properly. By providing interesting or entertaining content, you will more than likely entice people to view your video. If your videos offer quality content, they have a good chance of going viral and making you a lot of money. Have you ever received an email with a link to a video that moved you or made you laugh so you forwarded the link to someone you know? Well that is an example of "going viral."

If people like your video, if they find it moving or extremely informative or exceptionally funny, they will send the link to that video to people they know, either through email or by posting the link on the social networks. Video is so powerful—not only because of the sheer number of people who view video sharing sites every day, but because it can be much more persuasive than the written word.

Adding video to your Web site and marketing campaign is one of the smartest things you can do! Video captivates your readers, provides them with a warm welcome and keeps them on your site a lot longer so they are much more likely to take action.

Ideas for Types of Videos to Create

- Video tutorials
- Video FAQs
- Product reviews
- Book reviews
- A video welcome on your site
- Video interviews
- Video blog posts

How to Make Marketing Videos

Having a video on your Web site or blog is essential. It will create interest in what you are offering and people will be inclined to spend much more time on your site than they would have had you not had a video easily accessible.

Adding video to your Web site and marketing campaign is one of the smartest things you can do. Video captivates your audience, provides them with a warm welcome, and keeps them on your site a lot longer, thus they are more likely to take action.

Creating Web video can seem intimidating, while in fact it can be simple, affordable, or even free. Creating Web video can also be a lot of fun. You can either record your message with the camera facing you or you can create a screen capture video and record something that is on your computer screen.

You don't need to be a de Mille or Hitchcock to create your own videos for the Web. The technology has advanced to the point where it is easy to record a video, even if you're not a technology expert.

Webcam Videos

One form of Web video is where you are sitting at your desk and you turn on your Webcam and begin speaking. There is a lot to be said for this format. It is fast, easy, affordable, and effective. Your viewers get to know you and learn to like and trust you. You can set-up a Webcam right on top of your computer screen. This makes it really easy to get into the habit of recording a video at least once a week.

Before recording a video, you want to look behind you and see if it is clear, clean, and attractive. You do not want it to be cluttered, which can be distracting. You want people looking at you and paying attention to what you are saying. So you may need to be a little creative with your backdrop. One option is to have a solid colored wall behind you. Another option is to have an attractive oriental screen behind you.

Studio Videos

A much more involved method for creating Web video requires a studio setup. This can be a lot of fun and very effective but is definitely a lot more expensive and requires much more time, energy, and know-how. There is a technique called "green screen" which allows you to change the background images. For example, you can pop in an image that will give the illusion of you at the ocean, at the boardroom, on an airplane, or you can have a video behind you of people walking down the street. Newscasters use this method.

If you are industrious and like playing with software, you can use a green screen. You can have a sheet of either green paper or green fabric on the wall behind you. Make certain that there are absolutely no wrinkles in it. Shooting studio video requires that you have special and adequate lighting. It gives you a lot of flexibility. This is something that obviously is a more advanced technique but it's very doable.

If you want this level of video, you don't have to do it yourself. You can find local videographers who will charge a very reasonable fee to shoot and edit a short video. Post your project on Craig's List (www.CraigsList.com) for your area, and you will likely find a number of qualified candidates. You can also find inexpensive videographers through musical instrument stores and recording studios, as bands often need videos of their music and performances. If you go this route, be sure to interview candidates carefully. Ask for references and samples of their work.

Screen Capture Videos

Another very popular type of Web video is called screen capture video. This is where you create videos from content that is on your computer monitor. You can record a live Webinar, a PowerPoint presentation, a tour of a Web site or software program, and much more. One of the easiest ways to create a professional screen capture video is by using PowerPoint. Create your presentation, then open up Jing Project (for videos under five minutes in length) or Camtasia Studio (for longer videos) and record your video as you go through the slideshow. You will of course want to record an audio narrative to accompany your presentation.

Jing Project (www.JingProject.com) is a free screen capture video program from TechSmith that allows you to record up to five minutes of video. This is actually an ideal amount of time to get your message across and it makes it easy to upload to YouTube. Jing Project videos make great tutorial videos for your learning library. No fancy equipment is necessary. This platform is perfect if you have a client who is asking a specific question. If showing your computer screen will help in your explanation, then you can use this platform to do just that. Take a moment and download your free Jing Project software and make your first video today. You are going to love it and wonder how you ever lived without this tool!

If you fall in love with Jing Project and five minutes is not a long enough video for you, you may want to upgrade to Camtasia Studio (www.techsmith.com/camtasia.asp). This is not a free program but they do have a thirty-day trial period. With Camtasia Studio you can create videos of unlimited length and there's a lot you can do with the software. On the Camtasia Studio Web site you'll find dozens of tutorial videos that will walk you through every aspect of the program. Additionally you may want to enroll in Lon Naylor's Camtasia

course at (www.ScreencastVideoProfits.com). Lon
Naylor is a world-renowned expert on Camtasia
Studio. He not only provides you with the nuts and
bolts of using the program, he shows you how to add
your personality to your videos.

Once you've created your videos, you'll need a place
to post them.

YouTube: the Number One Video Sharing Site in the World

YouTube (www.YouTube.com) is one of the most
visited Web sites in the world and is considered to be
the second most accessed search engine in the world,
second only to Google. When people want to learn
something, they can simply go to YouTube and look
it up, the way many of us used to look for answers to
our questions in an encyclopedia.

The first thing you want to do is set up a channel on
YouTube. You can carry over your branded image
when selecting the colors and background for your
channel. You'll also want to make sure that your
blog is set up and that you have the proper plugins
installed, so that you can post videos right on your
blog. As you create videos, you can upload them to
both YouTube and to your blog. There are some very
powerful things you can do with your YouTube
videos such as ad text and callouts.

You want to have a branded YouTube station where
you can display your photo or logo. You can create a
user ID that represents your brand. People can view

your videos on YouTube and they can also embed them on their own Web site, thus giving you even more exposure.

Having a YouTube channel is a great way to grow your reach and your followers. Here are a few easy strategies that you can put in place from day one.

Once you have your YouTube station set up, your site design selected, and have added even one video, you can begin to grow your viewers and your friends. An easy way to do this is to search for other channels on your given topic. View a few of their videos and if you like their message and approach and believe that their content would be of value to your audience, add them as "friends" and subscribe to their channels. You will get viewers to your YouTube station as people will see that you are linked to channels that they subscribe to and they will want to check out your videos as well.

YouTube Video Tips

- When posting videos on YouTube, your videos should be between three and five minutes in length, and they must be under fifteen minutes. By keeping them within the three to five minute range people are more likely to view your videos in their entirety. This will make it more likely for them to embed your videos on their Web site so that their viewers can enjoy them.
- Since people are currently going to YouTube looking for specific content, any video content you produce should be available there. One

117

advantage of keeping your video content at YouTube is that it allows you to monitor how popular each of your videos are by seeing how many times they have been watched.

- Another great way to add value to your YouTube Station is to create a favorites section as well as a playlist of additional content that's going to be of interest to your viewers. YouTube is, in essence, a social network, an encyclopedia, and a marketing site all rolled into one.

- Once you have uploaded your videos to YouTube, you can add call outs and clickable text. Imagine being able to have an action step for people to follow such as "Click here to learn more."

UStream

To create a live broadcast television station, set up an account at UStream (www.UStreamTV.com). This is another free video site that you can brand with your colors and images or logo. You can either have a live TV show on any topic you'd like to share information on, or you can pre-record your show and upload the recording.

Webcam video is very effective for an online TV show. While your show is airing on UStream, you can elect to have a chat box available for your viewers. There are pros and cons to Ustream. There is a lot going on, on the site, in addition to your show, and viewers can easily become distracted and click off of your site. A major plus to Ustream, however, is that you can easily reach a wider audience, live.

Professional Looking Videos on Animoto

Visit Animoto (www.Animoto.com), where you are able to upload images and video, select music, and add text. It is a snap to create Animoto videos and they are highly professional looking. They provide the option for you to be able to upload your Animoto videos to YouTube. Make sure you have a YouTube account before you attempt to upload your Animoto videos. Once your Animoto videos have been uploaded to YouTube you will be able to share them with the world.

Video Blogging

Video blogging is quite simple and you can use a blog platform for your online Web TV station, your video newsletter, and/or your video tip of the week. A unique way to add video to your blog is to provide a way for your students or your clients to ask written questions. You can then answer those questions in video format and add those videos to your video training library.

Video captivates people and keeps them on your site longer. Setting up a video on your blog is very easy in WordPress. You have a couple of different options. First, create a video. Then upload it to YouTube. Once your video has been processed, you will be able to copy the embeded code to your blog in order to make the video play on a selected spot on your site.

When you're in the post-editing mode on your WordPress blog, you'll see that there is a place to put the code. Note that there is an HTML tab. Click on that tab and paste the video code into the HTML section and publish your post. When you do that you will have a video on your site.

Keep in mind that while YouTube is valuable for driving traffic to your Web site or blog, YouTube videos embedded on your Web site can divert people away from your site because when they click on your video, they are taken to YouTube. Additionally make sure when you copy the video embed code that you uncheck the "related videos" box.

The main reason for this is because it is possible for your competitors to upload a totally inappropriate video with the keywords that have to do with what you're interested in. You don't want your viewers watching pornography on your site. Just below the area where you uncheck the box for "related videos" you will see an option for border colors, which you can choose to match the branding of your site.

An alternative method involves setting up an account at Amazon S3 (http://aws.amazon.com). They do charge you for the bandwidth but it is ridiculously affordable. This way you keep your viewers on your site and prevent them from clicking off to YouTube. You will need to have a way to incorporate a video player with the AmazonS3 code. The premier Amazon S3 video player is called Easy

Video Player. It does require some technical know-how to set up the program, but once you do you'll be able to upload your videos in a matter of minutes. One of the beauties of using Amazon S3 and Easy Video Player for your video hosting is that you decide where the viewer will go at the end of the video and you are also able to decide if you want your video (or audio) to be downloadable. To learn about this method check out Easy Video Player (www.TryEasyVideoPlayer.com).

Another benefit of video blogging is that you can put a link to your video posts in your email newsletter and say something like: "Click here for this week's video." This is a great way to get a lot of traffic coming to your blog and Google is going to pay attention. It will increase your search engine rankings, which will get you more traffic.

To ensure that you have an ongoing source of new video content, consider scheduling a time each week to produce a few videos. This way you will have reserve content in case you want to take a vacation or you get busy with other projects. Create videos and you will be creating a powerful way to share your knowledge and your presence, while building relationships with your audience.

Action Steps

Here are seven steps that you can take to put what
you've learned into action.

1. Set up a YouTube account using your
   company's colors and images to brand your
   channel design.
2. Download a free copy of Jing Project.
3. Create a PowerPoint presentation which you
   can record and turn into a video.
4. Create a screen capture video with Jing
   Project and/or Camtasia.
5. Upload your video to your YouTube station.
6. Create an Animoto music/image video.
7. Add video to your blog/Web site.

Resources Mentioned in This Chapter

Craig's List: www.CraigsList.com

YouTube: www.YouTube.com

UStream: www.UStreamTV.com

Jing Project: www.JingProject.com

Animoto: www.Animoto.com

Camtasia Course: www.ScreencastVideoProfits.com

Camtasia Studio: www.techsmith.com/camtasia.asp

Easy Video Player: www.TryEasyVideoPlayer.com

Amazon S3: http://aws.amazon.com

Wrapping Things Up and Moving On From Here

In order to thrive in today's business environment, you need to set yourself and your business apart from your competitors. The most effective way to accomplish this is to build relationships with your prospects, clients and audience, and let them know you care.

- Use personal branding to become memorable.
- Develop your blog and treat it as the hub of your online empire.
- Participate on the social networks and become known as a giver.

- Consistently follow up to let your clients know you care and are there to help.
- Hold teleseminars on a regular or occasional basis and share your message.
- Repurpose your audio recordings into multiple forms of written content.
- Create effective, relationship building, Web videos that provide a way for people to get to know you.

It is essential to follow up with your clients. If you're not following up with them, how can you build a relationship with them? People have to remember you in order to refer you or do business with you. Consider incorporating a system that is easy for you to implement but will still impress the client. One of the examples mentioned was using a greeting card system to stay in touch with your clients and let them know you are thinking of them. Your clients will not only appreciate the gesture but will remember you for future projects.

Incorporate branding methods so that the public comes to recognize you and your business. A consistent color, logo or tagline will be remembered and will help your clients and potential clients to connect with you and your services.

Interact on the social networks and at in-person networking events and become known as a go-to person. Building long-lasting relationships will not only benefit you and your clients but also your business as a whole.

Building relationships, like building a business, takes time. Schedule time each week to develop your online presence and strengthen your business relationships. Your efforts and accomplishments will develop with consistent effort and attention and before you know it you will have a thriving, online, relationship marketing presence!

Resources

An integral part of Internet marketing is having the right tools for the job. Over the past decade I have had the opportunity to use many Internet marketing tools and resources. The resources mentioned in this book are ones that I personally use and highly endorse. Some of these services are free while others have either a free trial period or an ironclad satisfaction guarantee.

As an Internet marketer I do have an affiliate relationship with many companies, thus, if you do purchase a product through my affiliate link, I may receive a commission. As you discover resources that you use and recommend, you may want to see if they have an affiliate program. It's wonderful to be compensated for word-of-mouth recommendations. As you scroll through this list you may want to highlight the sites that you'd like to explore further.

Resources mentioned in this book:

Amazon S3: http://aws.amazon.com
Animoto: www.Animoto.com
Articles by Dvorah: www.ArticlesByDvorah.com
AWeber: www.WebmailConnections.com
Blitz Time: www.BlitzTime.com
BlogTalkRadio: www.BlogTalkRadio.com
Blog World Tour Planner: www.BlogWorldTour.com
Camtasia: www.techsmith.com/camtasia.asp
Craig's List: www.CraigsList.com

Easy Video Player: www.TryEasyVideoPlayer.com

Ezine Articles: www.EzineArticles.com

Facebook: www.Facebook.com

Free Conference Calling:
www.FreeConferenceCalling.com

Gmail: www.Gmail.com

Go Daddy: www.BestDomainPricing.com

Hoot Suite: www.HootSuite.com

Host Gator: www.WebHostingGator.com

InstantTeleseminar: www.WebTeleSeminars.com

Jing Project: www.JingProject.com

1ShoppingCart: www.BestShoppingCartSystem.com

Kunaki: www.Kunaki.com

Learn Camtasia Course:
www.ScreencastVideoProfits.com

LinkedIn: www.LinkedIn.com

Networked Blogs: www.NetworkedBlogs.com

Powerful Plugins: www.PowerfulPlugins.com

SendOutCards: www.CardsYouRemember.com

Twitter: www.Twitter.com

UStream: www.UStreamTV.com

VistaPrint: www.VistaPrint.com

Wishlist Membership Site Plugin:
www.WishlistMembershipPlugin.com

WordPress Themes by Studio Press:
www.ThemesbyStudioPress.com

YouTube: www.YouTube.com

Additional Resources:

www.AuthorsMarketingCircle.com
www.BookMarketingTeleseminars.com
www.BookMarketingGazette.com
www.HowToMarketYourNonFictionBook.com
www.BuildMyBlogPlease.com
www.RelationshipMarketingCafe.com
www.DropBoxExpress.com

Dr. Jeanette Cates – One Hour Training Series

www.YourOneHourMembershipSite.com
www.YourOneHourAffiliateProgram.com
www.YourOneHourShoppingCart.com

For further learning or to keep up to date with the *Connect, Communicate, and Profit* community, visit our resource center at: www.ConnectCommunicateProfit.com.

Acknowledgements

Ranan Lansky, my darling son, inspiration, and light of my life, may you discover your dreams and make them a reality. Looking forward to celebrating your first published book!

Attorney Rick Angel, my cousin and business partner, thanks for being an inspiration and my accountability partner. When we were kids we were inseparable. I'll never forget how they used to offer us a quarter if we could make it through dinner without giggling. I think we only got the quarter one time! It's so much fun to be able to be in business with you and be on this success journey together.

Gail Lapins, my dearest aunt, you have always guided me to live a life filled with joy, health, and prosperity. For the past fifteen years you have been my business advisor and confidant and I thank you with all my heart.

David Shaw, Dana and Bruce Kates, Rick, Shelli and Samara Angel, Uncle Aivars and Auntie Gail, Auntie Peggy, and Valerie—my loving and supportive family—thanks for always being there.

Sheila Schweit and Rich Leffler, my long-lost family members who have come back into my life, thank you for your love and friendship.

Reno Lovison, my mastermind buddy and dear friend, it is so much fun to brainstorm ideas and work on projects together. I appreciate you.

Kody Bateman, thank you for living your life with joy and love, listening to your promptings, and teaching others to do the same. I will be forever grateful for the SendOutCards opportunity and the many ways it has enriched my life.

Jordan Adler, thank you for your friendship and unconditional love. Your living example of excellence and positivity impact my life every day.

My amazing publisher, Alfred Poor of Desktop Wings Inc., you have been a delight to work with. Thank you for your ongoing encouragement and your belief in me. We'll get you that book series yet!

Marge and Bruce Brown, my mastermind partners, thank you for helping make my lifelong dream come true by introducing me to your publisher, Alfred Poor.

Kristen Eckstein of Imagine! Studios, thank you for doing such a spectacular job editing the manuscript, designing the book cover, and helping my book to shine.

Pamela Waldrop Shaw—who taught me pretty much all the most powerful things I know about being a successful, lead-by-example, network marketing leader—thank you for your love and friendship over the past decade!

Susan Maguire, thank you for giving me your business card, for your example of excellence, and for introducing me to Pam and the opportunity of a lifetime.

David Frey, you embrace the give-to-give philosophy. Thank you for reaching out and being so generous with your time and wisdom.

Bob "the teacher" Jenkins, you gave me the gift of a lifetime when you had me map out all my projects and put them onto a timeline. This has freed me up from distractions and multi-tasking and allowed me to accomplish so much. This book is living proof. Thank you for your friendship and mentorship.

Sara and Bobby Basloe, thank you for so wisely asking my cousin for a referral and then following up when he gave you my name. It is a joy to be on this success journey with you.

Mark Herdering, it meant the world to me that you reached out to offer encouragement and support when I was brand new in the business. Thank you for your friendship as well as your team spirit.

Linda Macedonio, thank you for inviting me to attend the BNI training those many years ago. You introduced me to my team leaders who represent more than 60 percent of my international team.

Sasha ZeBryk, thank you for being with me from the beginning of my success journey and for teaching me the fundamentals of the "Technicolor commercial." I appreciate you and value our friendship.

Cheryl Jones-Reardon, Dory Dzinsky, Joan Pagano and Sharon Massoth, enthusiastic students from my first internet marketing course, thank you for your encouragement and support. You are appreciated.

Noah St. John, thank you for sharing your powerful message of "afformations" and for being so "real." It is a joy and an honor to know you; thank you for your friendship.

To my amazing SOC Team Leaders who are living examples of our give-to-give philosophy: Susan, Gina, Leah, Joe, Dave, Scott, Pamela, Todd, Sal, Patti, Lori, Patty, Dave, René, Julie, Peggy, Jennifer, Lynda, Katie and Brennan, Tim, Debbie and Mike, Christine, David, Denis and Jocelyne, Richard, Yvon, Garnett, Chip, Jeff, Ralph, Bruce, Mecheal, Diana, Diane, Kacy, Carol, Phil, Becki, Sharon, Tamitha, Cindy, Kathy, Rahna, Sasha, and Bob. Thank you for your friendship and your example. What an honor it is to be on this journey with you.

Thank you to my SOC buddies and fellow leaders: Leann, Jimmy, DeMarr, Jordan, Mark, Sara and Bobby, Deb, Chad, Elliot, Michele, Casey, Elaine, Tommy, Curtis and Heather, Dave and Lori, Diane, Jack, Bob and Betty Ann, David, Frank, Tari and John, Phil and Sheila, Ben, Kristy and Scott, Jerry, Rick, Norm, Susan, Bob and Ellen, Amy, Judi, Kristi, Adam, Jeff, Jim and Sherry, Bart, Megan, Michael and Suzy, Aliza and Stephen, Maran, Michael, David, Penny, Steve, Janet and Al, Paul, Michael, Janalee, Clyde, Matthew and Jennifer, Dawn, Michelle, Michele, Kristy, Andrea, Judy, Kathy, Bill, John, Alan, Doug, Heidi, Bob, Chuck, Nicki, Sarah, Thomas and Stephanie, Tom, Tracey, Vonda, and Zoe.

Connie Ragen Green, whose example of heart-centered mentorship speaks louder than words, you are a living example of relationship marketing in action. Your lead-by-example approach to teaching and your incredible success pave the way for others to follow. Thank you for your friendship.

Dr. Jeanette Cates, your exceptional teaching style and expertise in your subject matter, as well as your obvious love for your students and for what you do, make it a joy and an honor to study with you.

Felicia Slattery, Nicole Dean, and Lon Naylor, thank you for being such incredible teachers and cheerleaders. I have greatly enjoyed learning with you and appreciate your encouragement and belief in me.

Anna and Jeff Hall, my new old friends, destiny brought us together and I am grateful for our connection.

Vicky and Drew Riggio, two heart-centered leaders who live the philosophy of Givers Gain, you have become extended family and success partners.

Sharon Stenger, Kathy McAfee, Rahna Barthelmess, and Patti Glick, my Monday Morning Mastermind, thank you for investing in my life and for bringing me my new motto, "Set Your Fun Meter on High."

Jessalyn Pito, Angel Johnstone and Michele Confessore, my DSWA sisters and fellow leaders, you have reminded me of how special it is to enjoy true and heart-centered friendship.

Marge Piccini, dear friend, thank you for your example of excellence and for your friendship. I will always hold dear in my heart our special birthday picnic at Elizabeth Park. Your brilliance shines as you teach others how to be brilliant in business and in life.

MaryAnn D'Ambrosio, Kay Kinder, Dave Francis, Erica Cosminsky, Marge and Bruce Brown, and Bob Lampard, my Fast Track Success Partners, thank you for spurring me on to higher heights and for the ongoing brainstorming sessions.

Becki Maxson, thank you for hunting me down over a dozen years from the date we were first in business together. Your friendship means the world to me, and the team you have developed has had a deep and positive impact on my life.

Donna Finocchiaro, your skills as a professional organizer have been a huge help to me over the years. Thank you for helping me to create a clear runway so that I can accomplish more with less effort. Your friendship is very special to me.

Rivereast BNI Chapter, you are an amazing group of networkers and friends. It is a joy to be able to support one another in growing our businesses.

Marilyn, Gordon, Allison, Tucker, Kate, Cameron, Danny, Zak, and Montana—my childhood family friends who have stayed in touch and been with us through every joy and sorrow—you have always been a very important part of my life.

About the Author

**D'vorah Lansky, M.Ed.
Author, Educator, Coach**

As a Relationship Marketing Wizard, I mentor business leaders and professionals across the globe to effectively and affordably market their businesses using online and offline relationship marketing strategies.

My work has appeared in *Chicken Soup for the Network Marketer's Soul, Corporate Mom Dropouts* and *Ignite Your Passion.* I am the executive producer of RelationshipMarketingCafe.com and an executive leader with SendOutCards. My independent distributorship can be found online at www.CardsYouRemember.com.

You can connect with me at:

- www.Twitter.com/marketingwizard
- www.Facebook.com/dvorah.lansky
- www.LinkedIn.com/in/themarketingwizard

I've always been interested in technology and remember my first computer. It had a 40 megabyte—yes, you read that correctly, 40 megabyte—hard drive which we didn't think we would ever fill up. When I first got started marketing online, it was back in the DOS days when you had to "disk park" to get your computer to turn off. I went from there to teaching myself how to build Web sites, program spreadsheets, and eventually build and design WordPress blogs. I built an international business where I connected and built relationships with people from around the globe. Back in those days I taught myself how to do all of this, as I was not aware of any courses being taught on these subjects.

I've gone on to continue my studies of Internet marketing. I've studied with some of the most successful Internet marketers in the world, including Armand Morin, Bob "the teacher" Jenkins, Connie Ragen Green, Dr. Jeanette Cates, Lon Naylor, Felicia Slattery, Nicole Dean, Andrew Lock, Frank Deardruff, Stu McLaren, and Tracy Childers.

What makes me unique as a marketer is that, in addition to my experience in Internet Marketing, I have been a leader in the network marketing industry for fifteen years and have more than ten years' experience with in-person networking. During that time I've been an active member and involved in various leadership positions in BNI, have participated in networking events with local Chambers of Commerce, and was a board member of our local DSWA (Direct Selling Women's Alliance) chapter.

I love people and I mentor business professionals, both one-to-one and in small groups via my online private and group-coaching programs. I also have an online radio show (www.RelationshipMarketingCafe.com) and offer

teleseminars and online training programs
(www.ConversationsAboutMarketing.com).

When asked what my special gifts are, I reply
"seeing the best in people and loving them to
success." The leadership position that I am in with
SendOutCards allows me the honor and privilege of
working with some of the kindest, most giving,
heart-centered individuals on the planet.

My dream is to continue to write books that provide
value and education and to exponentially grow my
business and my team. Someday soon, you'll find me
writing from the balcony of my dream home, a beach
house on the coast of California.

Now that you have a clearer understanding of how
to grow your business and strengthen your
relationships via relationship marketing, take some
time to outline a plan of action. Each week, choose
one or two things to focus on and you will be amazed
at how your business and your connections will
grow.

I'd like to personally invite you to enjoy a free
companion course where you will be provided with
the opportunity to connect, communicate, and profit
through relationship marketing. Turn to the next
page for details.

Here's to your success!

Dvorah Lansky

Here's Your
Free Companion Course:

Your First Seven Steps to Relationship Marketing Online

Congratulations, you now have the foundation for attaining relationship marketing success. Of the seven strategies that you've learned, blogging is the one strategy that my clients ask me to teach about the most. Thus, I've put together a seven part course to get you started with relationship marketing through your own blog.

Discover the secrets that some of the greatest sales people of all time have employed to create a loyal following, ongoing referrals, and customers for life.

Keeping in touch with your customers and prospects through an active blog will make them feel special and appreciated. This practice is one of the most powerful things you can do with regard to building business relationships.

If people know that the content they'll be receiving from you can help them to grow their businesses, they will make it a priority to read and listen to what you say.

Head over to the private member's area to gain immediate access to your course material.

Connect, Communicate, and Profit by Developing Your Online Platform

In this course I will take the mystery out of online relationship marketing through blogging.

You will learn how to:

1. Increase your visibility and gain exposure to new audiences with magnetic content.
2. Set up a professionally branded blog that promotes you as a leader in your field.
3. Discover ways to automate the functionality of your blog.
4. Make your blog easy to find with these search engine optimization secrets.
5. Engage your readers in conversations that lead to more referrals and sales.
6. Harness the power of popular Web sites to drive more traffic to your site.
7. Bring your offline clients into your online community.

Redeem Your Bonus At:

www.ConnectCommunicateProfit.com/secret7

LaVergne, TN USA
06 April 2011
223112LV00001B/181/P